Venture Capital Today

A guide to the venture capital
market in the United Kingdom

Tony Lorenz
Managing Director, Equity Capital for Industry

Woodhead-Faulkner · Cambridge

Published by Woodhead-Faulkner Ltd
Fitzwilliam House, 32 Trumpington Street, Cambridge CB2 1QY, England
and 51 Washington Street, Dover, NH 03820, USA

First published 1985

British Library Cataloguing in Publication Data
Lorenz, Tony.
   Venture capital today: a guide to the venture capital market in the United Kingdom.
   1. Venture capital—Great Britain
   I. Title
   332.63   HG5432

   ISBN 0-85941-275-X

Library of Congress Cataloging in Publication Data
Lorenz, Tony.
   Venture capital today.
   Includes index.
   1. Venture capital—Great Britain   I. Title.
HG5441.L67 1985   658.1'5224'0941   85-646

ISBN 0-85941-275-X

Designed by Geoff Green

Typeset by Hands Fotoset, Leicester

Printed in Great Britain by St. Edmundsbury Press, Bury St Edmunds, Suffolk

Contents

7091438

Part two: The venture capital spectrum

Part three: The investment process

Preface

This is neither a textbook nor a technical handbook, in the narrow sense of a Venture Capital Operator's Manual. Rather, it is a guide through the inexact, often subjective and rapidly developing new industry of venture capital in the United Kingdom.

There is no particular emphasis on technology in this book, although the provision of high-technology finance is a recurring theme. The book describes the size and structure of the UK venture capital industry today, the ways in which venture capitalists work, the stages of company growth and the appropriate form of venture capital to each. The structuring of investment packages, selection criteria and the role of the State are also discussed. Finally, a brief review is made of the current scene in other European countries and a few thoughts expressed about the future direction of the industry. It will be noted that there is no separate account of the venture capital industry in the United States, the pathfinder for all other countries. While reference is frequently made to US experience, to do justice to that subject would require another book. Several have been written already, and this book is focused directly on the UK industry – its past, present and future.

This general approach should, it is hoped, be of interest to the small business entrepreneur and to all those closely involved with him and his prospects. In particular, these include the clearing banker, accountant, solicitor and industrial consultant, as well as the entrepreneur's immediate family. Merchant bankers, stockbrokers and the City in general also have an interest in the later stages of venture capital as the 'exit' is approached. In addition, the venture capital arena is of relevance to the policy-makers – both politicians and civil servants.

The venture capital community includes many articulate, experienced and reflective practitioners who could well have written this book themselves. The author is perhaps fortunate in that he has had this opportunity of expressing his views, but in any young, growing industry, experiences differ and are in a continuing state of development.

In a general book such as this, describing the overall process of venture capital, it has been difficult to do justice to a number of key components of the process. Among these are the selection and aftercare of early-stage investments, how the entrepreneur and his adviser choose a venture capitalist, business plan preparation and the complex subject of valuation of young businesses, together with the structuring of investments. Each of these topics is worthy of a book in itself.

Many venture capitalists will agree on the key factors which will limit the growth of the industry; the availability of funds at the moment presents no problems, there continues to be a strong flow of suitable investment opportunities and there are (in the United Kingdom) well-developed exit mechanisms. Where the future is much less certain concerns the availability of trained venture capitalists, and whether the UK culture can produce sufficient trained entrepreneurial business managers. Only time will tell whether these last two factors will limit the success of the UK venture capital industry.

The media is beginning to play an important role in publicising the activities of smaller businesses in the United Kingdom and has focused on the potential of venture capital. The *Financial Times* has for some time featured a small business page, and specialist columns on these subjects are regularly provided in *The Times, Guardian* and *Accountancy Age*. There are also specialist small business magazines, including *Venture Capital Journal, Your Business, Venture UK* and *Venture Capital Report*. Business programmes on television are also beginning to highlight the world of the smaller business.

It must be remembered that many small businesses will achieve significant success without a penny of venture capital investment along the way. Many others will, however, benefit significantly from the contribution of venture capital – both through the investment provided and through the support and involvement of the venture capitalist. Venture capital is young, dynamic and as innovative in its processes and investment packages as are the companies in which it invests. There is a particular excitement at this time in being part of a new industry which promises to be flourishing strongly well into the twenty-first century.

March 1985   Tony Lorenz

Acknowledgements

First, a dedication to Bernice, my wife, and to my family for their patience and support during the writing of this book. Also, my grateful thanks to Sue Lawless, my secretary, whose commitment made this work possible. Further, I would like to thank other close friends for providing extra inspiration along the way.

Second, this book was only completed with a substantial contribution from a number of colleagues and friends within the industry. I would particularly like to mention Patrick Taylor, who cast an eagle eye over the Annexes on deal structuring, Brian Warnes for his help on the debt versus equity issue and Sue Lloyd for her help and advice. The British Venture Capital Association's proposals on executive share options and venture capital funds' taxation have been reworked and incorporated into the book – these were the combination of several experienced venture capitalists' views during my term of office as Chairman of the BVCA.

I am also indebted to Derham O'Neil, from whom many in the venture capital industry have learned much on the deal completion process, and to a number of accounting firms for most helpful information on the technicalities of the various exit routes for venture capital investments. Further, I would like to thank my colleagues at ECI for their continuing interest and encouragement and I hope this book has not raised unrealistic expectations of literary genius among them, nor among my friends in the industry!

Part one The UK scenario

1 Industry background and structure

The phenomenon

Background

Venture capital investment in the United Kingdom, and to an increasing extent in continental Europe, is at an unprecedented level of activity. A single, perhaps obvious, cause can be isolated. This is the belated but now widespread realisation that the future well-being of the mature European economies will depend, as never before, on the success with which the present dominance of old industries can be replaced by a thriving participation in the newer technologies and their supporting industries and services.

The worldwide recession which in the United Kingdom began in early 1980 brought to an abrupt halt the previous half-century's process of industrial aggregation and concentration. Suddenly, large industrial groups, which are generally committed to the older industries, found themselves with reducing demand, over-capacity, low margins and excessive manning. This poor situation was aggravated by a slowness to respond to what was, in effect, a permanent decline in their business base – rather than a temporary, cyclical trough. It is perhaps questionable whether, without the recession, it would have been realised so clearly that long-term economic survival had been at increasing risk over the past several decades.

The awareness of this serious vulnerability has caused industrial leaders, governments and major financial institutions to react in a variety of ways. Older industries are undergoing a rapid rationalisation, while the major companies already in the newer technologies are investing heavily to stay ahead in an increasingly international marketplace. In most high-growth areas, applied technology is led from North

America or Japan. The UK economy has long suffered from the paradox that, although in many important areas of research British science leads the world, British industry has historically been unable to develop and exploit this research lead by successful commercial application.

The Government has recently launched special financial incentive schemes for small companies and has increased the funding for product development programmes affecting many sectors of industry. State-controlled entities such as defence and the public utilities are funding research projects in partnership with private industry at a far greater rate than previously. Government-related research institutes are being encouraged to seek private-sector funding as never before.

With the decline of traditional industries and the consequent loss of opportunities for investment, the financial institutions, whether they be bankers, investors or advisers, are aware of the need in their own longer-term interests to seek out and support the newer industries. Because of the evident slowness of many large companies to respond to both the threat of accelerating erosion in their historical activities and the opportunities presented by the newer industries, it is generally recognised that a thriving small business sector is crucial for the healthy future of the UK economy.

In recent years much attention has been paid to the birth- and death-rates of new businesses. (For the first time, an encouraging if early trend can be discerned in the increasing net survival rate.*) Why are small businesses now showing signs of longer term viability? Undoubtedly, small businesses can be more flexible and fleet of foot in responding to external change, or internal weakness, than can large companies. However, they are also more vulnerable to pressures from their usually larger suppliers and customers, which can threaten their frequently fragile finances.

Perhaps the single most important factor behind the increasing survival of small businesses is the recent change in attitudes towards their financing. From the predominantly 'sink-or-swim' posture of only five years or so ago, government, lenders and major investors alike have all turned a substantial proportion of their energies towards providing more generous and specific funding packages for the smaller business. Additionally, many of today's small businesses are in the more modern

* Recent studies by Pom Ganguly of the DTI and by Gallagher and Stewart of Newcastle University.

industry sectors and thus have real in-built growth potential, albeit in highly competitive international markets.

Scope of venture capital

This book deals with a specific aspect of small businesses – the provision of risk capital so essential to their birth, survival and profitable growth. It is not concerned with short-term finance, overdrafts or loans – which are all banking instruments. While reference is made to the Loan Guarantee Scheme (Chapter 14), the book concentrates on the provision of permanent or equity-type capital, which in the smaller, private or unquoted business is known generally as venture capital.

Venture capital, as we know it today, is really a transatlantic expression imported into the United Kingdom in the 1950s. In broad terms venture capital means the investment of long-term, risk equity finance where the primary reward for its providers (the venture capitalists) is an eventual capital gain, rather than interest income or dividend yield. Another particular feature is that the venture capitalist usually has a continuing involvement in the business of the 'customer' after making an investment. This does not mean management interference, but a venture capitalist will seek to protect and enhance his investment by keeping close to the entrepreneur and his team in an active supporting role. This style of operation is in marked contrast to that of a banker or other lender. It also differs radically from the approach of a stock market investor, who can buy and sell at will, and rarely even meets the management of his investment. This approach is commonly known as 'hands-on' aftercare management.

A venture capital investment is illiquid, i.e. not subject to repayment on demand as with an overdraft or following a loan repayment schedule. The investment is realised only when the company is sold or achieves a stock market listing: it is lost when, as sometimes occurs, the company goes into receivership or liquidation. Venture capital is risk finance in the extreme.

The sources of venture capital are many and varied. They range from the entrepreneur's own savings, or those of relatives and friends, through Business Expansion Scheme funds, independent venture capital funds, equity arms of clearing banks (specialist subsidiaries providing equity-type financing packages), specialist departments of the savings institutions – pension funds and insurance companies – and include equity providers in the public sector, from both central and local government.

These sources may limit the form and size of venture capital they can

provide. Some will finance start-ups, some only later-stage or development capital; some will specialise in management buy-outs; and a
scarce few are prepared to fund research and development projects.
Many invest a minimum of £250,000 and few will provide venture
capital packages below £100,000. Upper levels are usually unlimited,
through the use of syndicates – a group of several venture capitalists.

Origins of the UK venture capital industry

Although it was not identified as such at the time, venture capital can be
seen in the fifteenth century with the merchant venturers who traded
internationally and established businesses in far-flung countries such as
India, Japan and other parts of South-east Asia. In many cases, these
initiatives took the form of armed expeditions, but often with funding
from wealthy private individuals who stayed in the safety and comfort
of their London, Lisbon, Paris, Madrid or Amsterdam palaces while
their entrepreneurs – the hardy sea captains – took the risks.

From these early steps grew such highly successful trading businesses
as the East India Company, which effectively controlled all trade in and
out of India for 150 years. Equally, the habit during the fifteenth to
seventeenth centuries of capturing prize ships from the competing
maritime entrepreneurs of other nations was a primitive form of take-
over battle, although with a greater spillage of blood than is usually the
case today.

This somewhat exotic past experience is, however, unrecognisable
when compared with today's venture capital scene. The foundations of
modern venture capital can be traced back to the late eighteenth
century and early nineteenth century, when inventors such as
Stephenson, Arkwright, Crompton and Brunel found wealthy private
investors to back their projects, many of which were essential to the
success of Britain's first industrial revolution.

During the nineteenth century, struggling inventors began to obtain
patronage from private individuals. By the mid-nineteenth century, the
process had become formalised with the launch of various companies to
build railways in parts of South America and the growing British
Empire, and to take on such high-risk projects as the construction of the
Suez Canal. For the first time these projects became companies whose
shares were traded by the emerging stockbroking industry. The investment trust movement dates from around these times, and it was
probably the Scottish investment trusts that first corralled private
funds into broad-based investment companies which funded a spread of

these high-risk overseas investment projects, as well as domestic enterprises.

The real development of venture capital, however – in the sense that it is generally understood today – did not begin until the 1930s, when Charterhouse was launched as the first modern professionally managed specialist fund, providing risk equity finance for young and growing small businesses in the United Kingdom.

Somewhat surprisingly, over the next 40 years the number of venture and development capital funds which survived more than a few years grew very slowly. By the mid-1970s, there were fewer than ten in active operation. For the most part, these were relatively small offshoots of much larger organisations, which included several clearing-bank groups as well as ICFC (Industrial and Commercial Finance Corporation) and Charterhouse.

For a brief period from the late 1960s until the stock market crash in 1973/74, the UK venture capital scene became more active, with probably twice as many funds in operation during that period. Many of these were sponsored by the leading merchant banks. For a variety of reasons, including the stock market crash and the oil-price crisis in the early 1970s, many of these funds either were wound up or became dormant.

The US venture capital industry, in its current form, really got under way in the late 1950s; it was largely a reflection of this a decade later that spurred the brief blossoming of the UK industry. The US industry also experienced a trough in the early 1970s, largely due, however, to the toughening of tax legislation which substantially reduced the amount of investor liquidity available for investment in the United States.

During the second half of the 1970s the US industry grew rapidly; by 1980, the pace in the United Kingdom had quickened as well with the formation of several new independent funds, including Equity Capital for Industry (ECI). There were further developments from larger organisations such as public utility pension funds, and the creation of semi-State venture capital bodies such as the National Enterprise Board and the Scottish and Welsh Development Agencies.

Present structure and size

By 1980, the number of active UK-based venture capital funds had doubled to around 20. Since then, the rate of growth in equity risk finance available for small business investment has become something of a phenomenon, with more than 80 new funds launched between 1980 and 1984. Where have all these funds sprung from? Who is managing them? How much finance are they able to invest? Perhaps most important of all – are they here to stay?

The United Kingdom's current 100 or more venture capital funds can be classified into five broad groupings based on parentage, ownership or source of funds:

(a) clearing-bank captive funds;
(b) funds sponsored by the savings and investment institutions, including those managed by the merchant banks;
(c) Business Expansion Scheme funds;
(d) corporate, academic and other private-sector funds;
(e) semi-State bodies (both central and local government).

As will be evident from Chapter 2, these broad categories are not always distinct, and there is much blurring at the edges, particularly as the competition has intensified in recent years. After all, each fund has the same overall aim: to identify and back the relatively few potentially successful entrepreneurs from among the many approaches it receives. Whatever the parentage or specialisation of a fund (see Chapter 3), they are all operating in the same general market.

In the early 1970s, the structure of the industry was much simpler, consisting almost entirely of bank-related funds. All the other categories have developed since then, with the Business Expansion Scheme (BES) funds, dating back to 1981 only, being the most recent. Table 1 summarises the approximate structure between 1952 and 1984.

Table 1. Fund management groups, 1952–84

	1952	1972	1975	1979	1984		
	No.	No.	No.	No.	No.	£m*	%
Clearing-bank-related (including 3i)	1	4	3	5	13	350	24
Institutionally backed							
Captive/semi-captive							
(including merchant banks)	1	9	3	5	27	600	42
Independents	–	1	3	6	30	280	20
BSS/BES funds	–	–	–	–	30**	90	6
Corporate/academic/other	–	2	2	3	6	20	1
Semi-state bodies							
(including local government)	–	–	1	4	10	100	7
Total	2	16	12	23	116	1,440	100

* Equity-type investments only.
** Management groups, not individual funds (total 73), and excludes stockbrokers', etc., in-house clients unless through funds. Some ten of these 30 BSS/BES funds are in management groups where there is also an institutional or bank-related fund.

Statistics on the number and amounts of venture capital investments in the United Kingdom are at present unreliable, and exclude the unquestionably large proportion of early-stage funding provided by the entrepreneur himself, or by private investors known to him. However, the figures in Table 2 are generally accepted as being of the right magnitude for the 'professional' industry, thanks to some excellent pioneering work by Venture Economics, publishers of the quarterly *UK Venture Capital Journal*. The figures on the funding currently available for equity-type risk investment are impressive, in the sheer magnitude of the recent growth in availability of this kind of finance.

Table 2. Venture capital investments, 1981–83

	1981	1982	1983	1984
		(Estimates)		
Number	194	281	340	450
Amount (£m)	66	63	80	140

Source: Venture Economics.

As in the United States, where nearly a third of all money raised by the venture capital community originates from pension funds, the UK industry owes much to the appetite of pension fund managers for venture capital investment (see Table 3). Individuals contribute a higher proportion than in the United States, at two fifths of all money raised, largely emanating from the Business Expansion and Start-up Schemes. Corporations are much less active in the United Kingdom, at 1%, than in the United States (12%), as are foreign investors, with 9% (16% in the United States).

Table 3. Independent venture capital funds – sources of finance, 1982–84

	%	
	UK	US
Pension funds	39	33
Private individuals	31*	18
Insurance companies	10	13
Investment trusts	2	–
Banks/merchant banks	4	–
Foreign investors	10	16
Corporations	1	13
Academic institutions/endowments, foundations/other	3	7
	100	100

* Business Expansion Scheme subscribers and private investors in public company venture capital funds.
Source: Venture Economics.

Table 4. UK/US venture capital activity comparisons, 1983–84

	US	UK	US/UK ratio
No. of funds	600	110	5.5
£bn committed	12.5	1.5	8.3
GDP (£bn)*	2,657	236	11.3
Population (million)	232	56	4.1

* Currency conversion at 1984 quarterly weighted average of £1 = $1.38 and GDP for US and UK in three quarters to September 1984.
Source: Venture Economics and trade estimates.

As yet, there has been little research into the rate of venture capital investment in the United Kingdom in comparison with the United States. The data shown in Table 4 highlight the relative youth of the UK venture capital industry, but the industry is already closing the gap by proportion in the amount committed and the density of funds – particularly when compared with the clear lead the United States has in GDP and population. These ratios should not be too closely examined, bearing in mind that the profile of the majority of UK funds is far from the typical US venture capital fund's style of operation. It would be a mistake, at present, to assume the UK industry could yet have as dramatic an effect on small business development as has been the case in the United States. Few UK funds make early-stage investments or are high-technology orientated, and many do not practise the 'hands-on' aftercare style so essential to the nurturing of young, growth businesses.

2 The players

As suggested in Chapter 1, the current venture capital 'players' in the UK industry can be placed broadly within one of five groupings, based on ownership or source of funds. No attempt is made here to comment qualitatively on these groupings, but a brief description of their history and distinguishing characteristics may be useful.

Clearing-bank captive funds

Except for Charterhouse, which can be identified as the United Kingdom's first modern venture in this field, dating from the 1930s, the joint-stock/clearing banks were the pioneering sponsors of mostly in-house or captive UK venture capital funds.

For many years, the United Kingdom's best-known small-business financing organisation has been ICFC, the Industrial and Commercial Finance Corporation. ICFC was an initiative of the Bank of England and the major clearing banks in 1945, formed as a consortium special-ising in the provision of long-term finance for small business. In essence, ICFC's main activity was that of providing long-term debt packages, often with equity investment in parallel. In 1956 ICFC took in Technical Development Capital (TDC) as its technology-orientated, venture capital arm. In 1983 ICFC became the ICFC Division of 3i (Investors in Industry). TDC is now known as the Ventures Division of 3i (3i Ventures), and is one of the United Kingdom's longer-established venture capital funds.

Midland Bank formed Midland Montagu Industrial Finance in 1968 in partnership with Samuel Montagu – at that time, before Midland acquired control, an independent accepting house. National West-minster launched County Bank in 1965 as a small companies loan and equity specialist. Williams & Glyn's sired National and Commercial Development Capital (NCDC) in 1970; and the Bank of Scotland originated Melville Street Investments via British Linen Bank, its merchant banking subsidiary, in 1972. It was not until 1979 that Barclays launched Barclays Development Capital, with Lloyds Bank's Pegasus Holdings emerging in 1981. Royal Bank of Scotland, the parent bank of Williams & Glyn's, also operated an independent equity financing arm during the 1970s.

Citicorp Venture Capital is one of two established foreign bank-sponsored venture capital funds, Citicorp being inspired by its highly successful US venture capital operation. Citicorp did have a UK venture capital operation from 1969–73, but the new initiative in 1980 has already become an active 'player' on the UK scene. Allied Irish Banks also has a UK venture capital offshoot of its Allied Combined Trust, Ireland's leading venture capital company.

A common feature of these bank-sponsored venture capital operations is that, unlike most independent funds which are closed-end (see below), they rarely have any limits as to funding, provided the parent bank continues to be committed to maintaining a venture capital activity. The funds involved usually represent a very small proportion of total group assets, profits and employees. The management team of a clearing bank's equity arm may include lending or merchant bankers from within the 'family', but usually also includes a core of specialists with outside venture capital experience.

The investment packages provided by such bank-sponsored funds will normally include a higher debt element and a greater emphasis on income-producing instruments than is the case with funds from non-banking venture capital groupings. The clearing banks and 3i are also the major conduit for the Government's Loan Guarantee Scheme (LGS) funds.

The £500 million provided to date under the LGS is filling a gap in the small business market, where few equity-type funds operate, i.e. in the £5,000–£75,000 requirement range. The LGS can, therefore, provide bank-sponsored venture capital funds with a quasi-captive deal flow, as the more successful LGS recipients grow to a size where equity funding in excess of £100,000 is required. (The LGS is covered more fully in Chapter 14.)

Clearing banks in the venture capital business have a wide coverage of the small companies market through their extensive branch networks, provided their branches are trained to identify smaller corporate customers with potential from among their many business clients. The

ICFC branch network is a highly effective sourcing facility, in terms both of access to the open market and of liaison with all the clearing banks branches in their territories.

Investment institution-backed funds

Increasingly, the major UK savings institutions – notably pension funds and insurance companies – have recognised the comparative, albeit long-term, investment opportunities presented by the smaller companies sector, particularly in the more modern industries. The majority of UK venture capital funds, both by number and by amount of equity finance committed, are now within this category.

To date, the institutions have invested largely indirectly, through the intermediary of independent funds managed by specialists in venture capital. These independent funds are further identifiable as *wholly independent* funds, which have their own management, and *semi-captive* funds, where one of the investors also provides the management team.

In recent years, some of the larger institutions have moved towards establishing their own *in-house* or *captive units*, as primary investors or 'owner-managers'.

Captive institutional funds

The first of these was the National Coal Board pension fund, whose direct equity investment arm is CIN Industrial Investments, started in 1976. Both British Rail pension funds and the Norwich Union have established specialist equity units since 1977. Britain's largest insurance group, the Prudential, set up its own venture capital unit during 1984, as well as launching Prutec – its wholly owned high-technology fund. A number of the other major insurance groups have participated in 'DIY' venture capital investment, albeit without distinct in-house units.

These major institutions with in-house units also often have one or a number of minority investments in independent venture capital funds which may compete with each other as well as with the in-house units of the independent fund's own investors.

The institutional investor in venture capital will usually allocate either a fixed initial amount to this activity or, alternatively, a stated percentage of the annual cash flow. For example, CIN Industrial Investments has publicly declared its aim of allocating 15% of its £400 million annual cash flow to venture capital investment. Whatever the resultant figure, this is likely to cover both in-house and external 'intermediary' funds. Similarly, the Prudential's captive venture capital arm, Pruventure, has publicly announced an annual target of £15 million investment in UK unlisted companies.

Captive institutional fund management usually consists of a mixed team of external recruits from industry, consultancy or the accounting profession, together with some of the fund's own personnel from its quoted portfolio.

The investment packages from captive institutional venture capital funds are generally largely equity-based, involving lower proportions of debt than with clearing-bank-related funds. There is, however, likely to be a greater emphasis on running yield (dividend income) than is the case with most independent funds, probably because of the stronger influence of actuarial constraints which require an income flow to match future liabilities to policy-holders and pensioners.

Captive institutional funds seek their investments from the open market. They rarely have a 'tied' market like that of the clearing banks. There are, however, special links with the City's merchant banking and stockbroking community. This is through the equity and gilts portfolio dealing which constitutes the dominant activity of savings institutions, where the latter are the major customers of stockbrokers and merchant banks' investment management teams. As many a venture capital proposal appears first on a stockbroker's or merchant banker's desk, there is a natural reciprocity in the proposal being offered first to their institutional clients.

Independent venture capital funds

The independent fund in the UK venture capital industry today can take various forms. The common feature is that no one shareholder or investor has a dominant position in the fund's ownership. Where a fund has a management team independent of any of its investors, it can be regarded as *wholly independent*. Where one of the investment partners supplies the management, it is defined here as *semi-captive*.

Semi-captive funds often arise where a merchant bank or other investment management group has established its own in-house fund and at some stage invites a number of its investment clients from among the savings institutions to join the fund.

A number of well-known merchant banks have now launched such funds. These include Hill Samuel's Fountain Development Fund, N. M. Rothschild's Biotechnology Investments, Hambros Advanced Technology Trust, Schroder Wagg, Kleinwort Benson, Lazards, Charterhouse Japhet and Barings.

Among specialist investment management groups to have established venture capital funds are Gartmore, with Cayzer Gartmore Investments and English & Caledonian; Foreign and Colonial, with FACET (Foreign and Colonial Enterprise Trust); Murray Johnstone, with Murray Technology, Murray Electronics and Murray Ventures; and Cazenove, with Newmarket and Baronsmead.

Wholly independent funds are usually started by a group of experienced individual venture capitalists seeking financial backing from several investment institutions. More rarely, this kind of fund is formed following the initiative of one or more institutions, which then jointly seek an experienced team to manage the fund.

Examples of the latter approach are Equity Capital for Industry (ECI), formed in 1976 by a wide variety of institutions which then recruited a management team, and Managed Technology Investments (MTI). More usual is the formation of Abingworth, Advent, APA Associates, Lovat Enterprise Fund, Venture Founders and Thompson Clive, where in each case institutional backers were approached by the fund's management teams.

These wholly independent funds are usually closed-end (having a specified initial capital base) and are primarily equity-orientated, seeking a long-term capital reward rather than an income flow from regular dividend payments. Often the funds are established with a maximum life of, say, ten years. They are then liquidated and the proceeds distributed to investors and managers in some pre-agreed proportion. This approach is similar to that of the US venture capital industry.

Most independent funds are characterised by other US venture capital features, such as a degree of technological specialisation and a 'hands-on' approach to management. This direct involvement of the venture capitalist in the aftercare of his investee companies is a relatively recent phenomenon in the United Kingdom, and is discussed in Chapter 10.

The management teams of independent funds, in both the United Kingdom and the United States, are usually headed by 'senior' venture capitalists who have gained their investment experience elsewhere. These teams generally include people with industrial management experience, as well as some with financial investigatory skills.

Technological specialisation, if any, is covered either by recruitment from the industry sectors concerned or by establishing a panel of reputable technical advisers from universities, industry and research organisations – or possibly by a combination of the two.

In the funds where management is wholly independent of the institutions providing their finance, it is now common practice to provide incentives for the management through a scheme allowing them to share in the fund's overall success – wins and losses included. This practice is much more difficult to achieve in the semi-captive and captive funds, where the parent or sponsoring organisation has other activities whose managements are not, or cannot be, encouraged in such a way.

Independent funds seek their investments from the open market in general, although those with particular technological links to academic or research establishments can develop a skill and reputation in those technologies, giving them a 'first port of call' cachet in the market-place.

Semi-captive funds may also have a 'preferred' investment flow from sister activities within, e.g. a merchant bank's corporate finance or lending business.

An important feature of the more successful independent funds, which are the most exposed in terms of both their clear capital performance requirement and the isolation from their backers, is the ability to generate their own investments by identifying suitable opportunities before the general market is aware of them.

Business Expansion Scheme funds

The role of the State in venture capital is described later in this chapter and in Chapter 14. The most important recent innovations in small business finance initiated by the Government are the Loan Guarantee Scheme (LGS) referred to earlier and the Business Expansion Scheme (BES), formerly the Business Start-up Scheme (BSS).

Although the origin of the BES is in statutory legislation, the finance is directly subscribed by individual private investors. Further, the approved funds which manage these private investors' venture capital portfolios are almost exclusively private sector in nature, style and objective.

By March 1985, there were over 70 approved BES and BSS funds in operation, with a total amount subscribed of over £100 million. Because of the annual nature of the tax offset to private investors, this amount was largely fully committed at March 1985.

Originally, the BSS was defined so as to concentrate on new businesses, specifically those less than five years old. Partly because of the failure of this scheme to attract adequate funds (£15 million subscribed in two years of the £100 million minimum expected by the

Government), the BES rules were widened to enable investment in well-established businesses, including those traded in over-the-counter share markets but not in the Unlisted Securities Market (USM).

The management teams responsible for BES funds are found among a variety of financial institutions. The leading BES fund, Electra Risk Capital (ERIC), is managed by a unit of Globe, the largest investment trust group in the United Kingdom. Some have been launched by stockbrokers, including Laurence Prust, Laing & Cruikshank, Hoare Govett, Parsons, and Buckmaster & Moore. Others derive from merchant banks, such as Charterhouse Japhet, Lazards, Guinness Mahon, British Linen Bank, Singer & Friedlander, Warburgs and County Bank. A number are managed by small independent investment teams such as Granville & Co., Capital Ventures, Hodgson Martin, Baronsmead and Centreway.

An increasing number of BES investments are made on a one-off basis by professional financial advisers throughout the country, who can bring together wealthy private clients and small business clients seeking finance. Accountants, solicitors and stockbrokers are becoming actively involved as 'matchmakers' to BES deals.

The BES funds' sources of investments are similar to those of most other venture capital funds; as a result, the subsidised cost of investment implicit in the BES represents a competitive threat to other banking- or institutional-related venture capital funds.

Undoubtedly, the BES has attracted much interest since its launch in mid-1983. There remain, however, drawbacks to the present BES rules which place serious constraints on the scope of this reawakening of private investor interest in venture capital. These and other BES issues are discussed further in Chapter 14.

Corporate and other private-sector funds

Unlike the United States, the United Kingdom has few venture capital funds backed by established quoted companies, by wealthy private individuals or by private foundations. In the United States, the proportion of all venture capital investment from these sources was more than 20% in 1983 (12% from endowments and/or foundations and 8% from corporations). Some of the largest US venture capital funds are of corporate or private foundation origin.

The *corporate venture capital* habit does show some signs of percolating slowly across the Atlantic, however, with major companies such as Plessey and Monsanto participating in the recent launches of Advent

Technology and Advent Eurofund. Since the early 1970s, a few major UK corporations have operated venture capital activities through specialised in-house units – namely Shell, BP and BOC (British Oxygen). Among smaller companies which have been involved are Crest Nicholson and Centreway Trust.

The prime motivation for corporate venture capital is usually either (or a combination of) relatively low-risk diversification or potential access to technology in similar or peripheral fields of activity.

Venture capital units within a large corporation are generally staffed by their own 'fast track' senior or middle managers as part of the latter's management development. The ideas and projects they pursue arise from within the organisation, from unsolicited approaches by entrepreneurs and, increasingly, from potential joint-venture partners in the venture capital industry, usually among the independent funds.

Private foundation venture capital investment in the United Kingdom is rare. Two such funds are Innotech, the Sainsbury family venture capital vehicle, and Capital Partners International, a German/Swiss family enterprise.

The basic motivations for private foundations and similar groups to invest in the venture capital industry are not always easy to identify. They can be a form of philanthropy, diversification of the family portfolios, the personal leanings of family members or any number of other motivations.

Usually, the family itself will exercise a significant degree of control over investment and divestment decisions, but their foundation will often employ a small team of experienced venture capitalists as full-time management. Other than through the Business Expansion Scheme, it is unlikely that the United Kingdom will see as active a participation in venture capital by family foundations or other private wealth sources as in the United States. Wealthy families in the United Kingdom are more cautious, preferring safe investments once their wealth is achieved. (After many years of supertax, there are also far fewer of them.) And their wealth is 'old' in the main, with the original entrepreneurial flair having been diluted in the family genes over the decades.

A recent development in UK venture capital has been the entry of *science-based universities* into the industry – both indirectly through investment in independent venture capital funds, and directly through the establishment of science parks linked to their science faculties. The science park concept has spread from the United States; recent UK initiatives of this type are in Cambridge, Birmingham (Aston University), Warwick and Edinburgh (Heriot Watt). In a number of cases the university has invested in its science park as a corporate entity, jointly with venture capitalists. In other cases the university simply provides the facilities and special access to its research resources for companies that rent space in the science park. UK venture capital funds, particularly those specialising in advanced technology, are becoming increasingly involved in science park-based companies as potential investment vehicles.

A further source of UK venture capital projects is the wide range of *research bodies and institutes*, some public sector, some private. Several of these have formed links with individual venture capital funds; others have preferential ties to public-sector initiatives such as the National Research and Development Corporation (NRDC), Celltech (linked to the Medical Research Council) and Agricultural Genetics (linked to the Agricultural Research Council). A different form of linkage is where a specialist venture capital intermediary acts as a channel for projects from independent research bodies to host companies. Such an organisation is Cogent, backed by two major insurance companies, Commercial Union and Legal & General.

There is a similar impetus for both universities and research institutes to participate in venture capital investment, namely the commercial exploitation of their key assets – research or intellectual property, as it is frequently described. Among the van of such venture capital-orientated universities are Cambridge (particularly Trinity College), Aberdeen (through its AURIS vehicle), Manchester/Umist (Vuman) and Imperial College, London, with a number of offshoot exploration companies. The SERC (Science and Engineering Research Council) sponsors university staff working alongside technology-based companies; the ACARD (Advisory Council for Applied Research and Development) is discussing with the DTI special grants for academic institutions that carry out research useful to industry; and the Committee of Vice-Chancellors and Principals has significantly enhanced the role of University Industry Liaison Officers by setting up an Industry Committee.

In the recent past, both universities and research bodies have come under pressure from government to reduce their financing burden on the State. Simultaneously, the UK venture capital industry has now blossomed on a scale providing these bodies with realistic opportunities to sell, license or 'joint-venture' their ideas and research projects to the general benefit of their organisations and, increasingly, to the particular benefit of their individual research teams. Undoubtedly, this academic participation in the venture capital industry will grow as a frequently more satisfactory route than the previously available alternatives of either working with large corporations or arranging transatlantic technology transfer for a licence fee and royalties.

There are also encouraging signs that university and research faculty members are themselves prepared to become technological entrepreneurs by applying their own research in companies specifically formed for the purpose – with or without initial participation by professional venture capitalists.

Semi-State bodies

Since the mid-1970s, the State has become more closely involved in venture capital in two key areas: first, by introducing aid schemes and legislation favourable to the small-business sector (especially the Loan Guarantee Scheme and Business Expansion Scheme); and second, by setting up national or regional State-owned financing institutions.

The wider role of the State in promoting venture capital is discussed in Chapter 14, where the various types of special aid, grants and schemes available are outlined. The following is a brief overview of the State-owned agencies directly active in the venture capital industry.

Central government

The first major State initiative in the UK venture capital industry was the launch in 1949 of the National Research and Development Corporation (NRDC). The primary objective of the NRDC was to promote the transfer of technology from Britain's universities and science-based research institutes to the corporate sector. A similar function was the joint-venturing of private-sector projects, both with individual investors and with established companies. This initiative was carried out with some notable successes such as cephalosporin, pyrethroid insecticides, hovercraft, etc.

The National Enterprise Board (NEB) was formed in 1975 with a wide-ranging role to finance high-risk equity ventures – both advanced technology start-ups and turnarounds, and rescues of established companies in more traditional industries. In 1980 the NEB was merged with the NRDC, the other State-owned high-technology financing institution, to form the British Technology Group (BTG).

The BTG has undergone a fundamental change since 1982, with the cessation of its more entrepreneurial NEB role and a concentration on the NRDC role of technology transfer, licensing and joint ventures with individual investors and with industry.

The BTG has also lost its exclusive right of access to universities and government research bodies, which are now free to exploit their projects directly in partnership with private-sector funds. The BTG's future role is therefore likely to be a less influential one than hitherto, particularly in the advanced technology sectors.

The Scottish, Welsh and Northern Ireland Development Agencies play an active role in start-up, expansion and turnaround venture capital within their geographical regions. They have their place in providing seed capital as well as physical facilities (factories and warehouses) for companies not yet at the stage where private-sector venture capital is available. The SDA, WDA and NIDA also have a major regional role in attracting large companies' expansion or relocation projects, both from other parts of the United Kingdom and from overseas.

Local government

A second tier of State-owned venture capital-type funds has developed since 1982. Largely as a result of the recession and the loss of employment prospects in older industrial areas, local government has established a variety of enterprise boards, development funds and similar agencies. Usually financed by local ratepayers' money, together with local authority employees' pension funds, the aim of these agencies is primarily to attract new employers to the area, whether they be new companies or established businesses. Another role lies in supporting existing local businesses experiencing trading difficulties.

While many of these local government agencies' operations are not in venture capital, a number have operated as venture capitalists at least in part of their activity, notably the West Midlands Enterprise Board, Merseyside Enterprise Board, Greater Manchester Development Fund, West Yorkshire Enterprise Board and Greater London Enterprise Board.

The British Venture Capital Association

In January 1983 the British Venture Capital Association (BVCA) was formed, with a founder-membership of 33 funds and current membership of 60 funds. This initiative developed from the UK Venture Capital Forum, which was an informal club of venture capitalists started in late 1980 by Equity Capital for Industry (ECI), Midland Bank Venture Capital and Citicorp Development Capital (now Citicorp Venture Capital). Over the two-year life of the Forum, the regular lunch-time

gatherings of the 'club' had grown to include some 18 active participants in the flourishing UK venture capital movement.

The Forum had provided a regular venue for an exchange of ideas
and deals, and a voice for the industry to legislators and policy-makers
in areas affecting venture capital in general. It was a growing realisation
of the potential effectiveness of this common voice, together with
pressure from within the membership, that led to the formalisation of
the Forum. The establishment of the BVCA was welcomed by the then
Minister for Small Businesses, John MacGregor, and other financial
authorities.

The main objectives of the BVCA are to:

(a) act as a focus of members' views and interests in discussions with
government, financial and regulatory authorities, and other trade
or professional bodies;
(b) provide a regular forum for the exchange of views among members,
with the idea of encouraging joint investment participation in
projects and of providing further stimulus to the UK venture
capital industry; and
(c) develop and maintain the highest standards of professional practice
and ethics among member companies with substantial funds at
their disposal for investment in venture capital projects.

Membership of the BVCA is open to professionally managed venture
capital funds investing equity stakes in unlisted companies. Members
include the leading funds set up under the provisions of the Government's Business Expansion Scheme, funds specialising in high-
technology start-ups, and those involved in second-stage financing and
in the field of management buy-outs. Though most of the funds in
membership are privately managed, the public sector is also represented. The BVCA membership includes the majority of funds, both
by number and by amount committed, active in UK equity-type
venture capital investment. In total, it is estimated that the BVCA
members have equity finance available in excess of £350 million to
encourage and enhance the growth of the smaller British business, and
a total amount already invested of some £550 million.

The BVCA has continued the Forum's practice of holding regular
meetings, usually monthly, some involving outside speakers and guests,
some open to members only. Development of the series of meetings held
with Government ministers in the Forum's era has been continued by
the BVCA Council, whose submissions to the Government for fiscal
and other changes to enhance the efficiency of the venture capital

industry have produced encouraging results at such an early stage in the BVCA's existence.

At present, the BVCA membership is not structured into special interest groups. It is to be expected that as the membership grows there will be a natural concentration, under the BVCA umbrella, among common-interest funds such as the Business Expansion Scheme members, those involved in management buy-outs, and the high-technology and start-up specialists.

A progress report on the achievement of the BVCA's main objectives could be summarised under the following headings.

Members' forum

While the BVCA does not monitor in detail the specific investments made jointly as a result of the BVCA's regular gatherings, undoubtedly there is a stimulus to syndication among members from the existence of these events. There is also a grass-roots consensus which emerges on a variety of subjects, enabling the Council to represent BVCA views externally, both to the authorities and to the Press.

Legislative influences

Formal submissions have been made since the BVCA began in early 1983 on subjects regarded by the membership as important to the promotion of entrepreneurism in the United Kingdom, and on the fiscal efficiency of the structure of venture capital funds. In particular, recommendations were successfully made to remove the extreme tax penalties attached to executive share options for managers of smaller businesses, and to improve the fiscal treatment of venture capital funds – where currently there is dual taxation for investors on the successful realisation of investments. Other areas where submissions have been made are the improvement of mobility for executive pensions and increased flexibility in BES rules.

Professional standards

There is now a published code of conduct for BVCA members, which will bring some formality to the membership's professional standards.

An important feature of the BVCA's activities is an annual con-ference, open to the investment community in general and to the entrepreneur, without whom the venture capitalist could not exist. In December 1984 the second such conference, jointly sponsored by the *Financial Times* and BVCA, was held. The objective of these confer-ences, believed to have been the first of their kind in Europe, was to enable entrepreneurs seeking finance, then or at a later stage, including those planning an over-the-counter, USM or full stock market listing, to present their companies to a broad spectrum of potential investors – venture capitalists, merchant bankers, investment managers, stockbrokers and others.

At present, the BVCA is deliberately not set up as a clearing-house for venture capital propositions, but members of the BVCA will usually be able to suggest sources of finance to entrepreneurs who approach them if the fund originally approached is not itself able to invest. A list of major UK sources of venture capital is included in Appendix A.

3 The players' specialisms

Most UK venture capital funds operate with some degree of special-isation in the investments they seek or are prepared to consider. These specialisms are based on:

(a) the state of development of the investee company, which defines the financing stage as perceived by the venture capitalist (see Part Two, Introduction, Table 5);
(b) the fund's investment size range;
(c) the preferred financing instrument and particular reward mix, i.e. income or capital growth;
(d) the fund's technological focus, if any;
(e) the timescale to realisation; and
(f) any geographical limitation.

The first item concerns the various stages of venture capital financing, related to the investee company's state of development. These stages are fundamental to an understanding of the whole spectrum of venture capital, and are described in Chapters 4, 5 and 6. The other specialisms among venture capital funds are discussed in this chapter.

Size of investment

The players in the venture capital market-place do not all invest in a similar size of company, nor do they all operate within a common range of amount invested. The minimum/maximum equity percentages also vary from fund to fund.

Although there is no real stratification of the market but rather a continuous progression of size preferences, there is a clear separation at either end of the size spectrum. For example, few funds are prepared to invest ·in amounts below £100,000 equity per transaction, since the economics of running a professional fund with any degree of 'hands-on' involvement do not easily accommodate such relatively small transactions. Equally, few funds are prepared to take a majority or controlling equity position from the outset.

These two factors combine to ensure a real gap for the smaller businesses. This gap is currently filled to some extent by the Loan Guarantee Scheme, but the LGS provides debt, not equity – which has its own dangers, as discussed in Chapter 12.

At the upper end of the spectrum – above, say, £1 million transaction size – there are also few funds that will invest as 'solo' participants. Typically, such larger transactions are covered by syndicates of at least two investors. Often three or more are involved but, as the number of syndicate partners grows, so does the difficulty of reaching a common agreement on deal structure, investigation responsibility and post-investment aftercare.

The UK syndication scene is not yet as advanced or sophisticated as it is in the US venture capital industry, where the leader of a syndicate is usually given full discretion by his partners to investigate, negotiate and provide aftercare. Such smooth syndication must also develop in the United Kingdom if the market is to operate effectively. Syndication is discussed further in Chapter 9.

Most venture capital funds invest in the range of £250,000 to £750,000 per transaction. It is unusual for any fund's eventual equity holding (including conversion of any convertible stock) to be less than 10% or more than 40%. Syndicates, however, frequently have combined holdings in the range of 40–80%, particularly at the upper end in larger management buy-outs (see Chapter 6).

The size of the investee company in sales, assets, profits or employees is not normally the deciding factor in the investment size preference of different funds. Basically, the fund's rate of return criteria, minimum/ maximum equity percentage limits and the amount of funding required will dictate the valuation of the company – which itself depends on the size of the business as defined by profitability rather than turnover, assets, employees or any other factor. If the amount required gives the fund too small or paradoxically too large a share of the equity (if this results in a controlling position), on a realistic valuation, then the fund is unlikely to invest.

Naturally, in early-stage financing (see Chapter 4) the investee company is rarely profitable, and the venture capitalist's valuation will normally be based on profitability at some future date. The outcome, with regard to transaction size and equity holding, all flows from the prospective profitability, just as actual profitability dictates the valuation for established businesses. Some funds, particularly those active in later-stage financing (or development capital), seek a minimum level of achieved profitability in a potential investee. The figure most often quoted is £100,000 pre-tax profits.

Financing instruments and reward mix

Equity investment, the core of any venture capital transaction, can involve one or more of a wide range of financing instruments. These include, in decreasing order of risk, the following:

(a) *Deferred (ordinary) shares*, where the ordinary share rights are deferred for a period of years or until some future event such as a quotation or sale of the company.
(b) *Ordinary shares*, with full equity and voting rights from the outset but no dividend commitment.
(c) *Preferred ordinary shares* (or 'B' ordinary shares), usually with full voting and equity rights, but often with a modest fixed dividend right and possibly also with right to *profits participation*.
(d) *Preference shares*, which rank ahead of all types of ordinary shares on a liquidation. As with deferred shares, preference shares may be wholly or partly *convertible* into ordinary shares at some future date or event. They may be *irredeemable* or more frequently *redeemable*, either at par or at a premium. The dividend may be cumulative and often can be increased through *participating* in future profits, usually once an agreed threshold is reached. Convertibility will often be at a variable rate depending on profits performance over a period of years giving the entrepreneur a strong incentive to achieve his forecasts made at the time of investment.
(e) *Convertible loan stock*, which is debt, usually long-term (over five years) until converted into ordinary shares, as with convertible preference shares. This type of loan stock, unlike conventional debt, is usually unsecured, possibly subordinated to all creditors, and bears either a fixed rate of interest or a margin over LIBOR (London Interbank Offered Rate).

In addition to these equity instruments, venture capital funds are sometimes prepared to provide conventional loans, hire-purchase, leasing and even overdraft finance – always, however, in combination with an equity-dominated package.

A number of bank-related small-business financing organisations specialise in providing medium- and long-term 'patient' (less secured and with 'softer' covenants than conventional loans) debt packages, but may also seek an equity option or 'kicker'. In this type of financing and where debt instruments dominate a transaction package, we are no longer in the world of venture capital; a detailed discussion of debt instruments is not, therefore, relevant here.

Among the equity instruments referred to are various combinations arising from the nature of the particular financing, e.g. start-up, buy-out or expansion finance. Examples of these combinations are given in the Annexes beginning on page 175 which relate to Chapter 4 (Early-stage Financing), Chapter 5 (Later-stage Financing) and Chapter 6 (Buy-outs).

As to individual preferences by fund, there are few generalisations which can be made. Unlike the stock market, which has a straight-forward 'off the peg' approach to providing new equity for quoted companies, venture capitalists as a rule design each transaction package to suit the specific requirements of the proposition. The state of development of the investee business is of key importance, as is the attitude of the entrepreneur to the scale of dilution of his equity and ownership. Such packages can be almost infinitely variable in their content but will always include significant equity rights, even if other elements like redeemable preference shares and loan stock are involved.

If any patterns do emerge, they are likely to be related to the type of fund. *Business Expansion Scheme* funds are prohibited by law from investing in other than ordinary shares. *Bank-related* funds are likely to have a substantially higher proportion of debt instruments in their transaction packages than do other types of venture capital funds. Most *institution-related* funds have higher proportions of ordinary and pre-ferred ordinary shares in their packages, but will often include fixed-interest redeemable preference shares as well as participation rights.

The US-style *independent* funds and *early-stage high-technology* funds are likely to have ordinary shares and preferred ordinary shares dominant in their packages, since their prime objective is to maximise the long-term growth of their equity rather than to achieve a mix of current income and future capital gain.

State-owned funds are more likely to include 'specials' such as grants, rates subsidies and 'soft' loans. Their equity requirements are often less onerous than those of private-sector funds, since their objectives are usually, at least in part, to create or preserve jobs rather than to maximise their long-term capital gain.

Technological focus

High technology or 'high tech' is a catch-phrase today. In the 1980s almost every newly quoted company, whether in the USM or the full stock market, claims to be 'high tech' in some respect – even companies with several decades behind them, operating in traditional products, which are 'into the latest advanced technologies'.

In reality, many UK companies are applying the latest advances in technology from the United States, Japan and West Germany to their own manufacturing processes or product developments. Few are new companies operating at the leading edge of important new technologies, on an internationally competitive basis.

There is, however, increasing evidence of successful start-ups by experienced, technically trained entrepreneurs who have left their large company employers to branch out on their own. Frequently, these start-ups are achieved without a venture capitalist. Most venture capitalists do not claim to specialise only in high-technology investments, although their portfolios may well include a significant proportion of businesses which operate in areas of advanced technology.

There are, however, a number of venture capital funds which deliberately set out to concentrate on advanced technology investment. Most of these are recently established, including Prutec, Advent, Innotech, MTI (Managed Technology Investments) and N. M. Rothschild's Biotechnology Investments. TDC, now renamed 3i Ventures, has invested in high-technology propositions for more than a decade. The NRDC arm of the BTG (British Technology Group) has been established for even longer – more than 30 years.

Undoubtedly, there is a new breed of UK venture capitalists emerging, originally from the advanced technology industries, who can actively partner technical entrepreneurs in those industries and who can also create new businesses from concepts and pure science programmes in UK universities and research institutes. This is a phenomenon of the 1980s in the United Kingdom, although it has been relatively common in the United States for 20 years or more.

There is a relatively small group of funds, mostly independent, which have a mix of high tech and more traditional industrial sectors in their portfolios. They will have some of the skills of high-tech funds, will adopt a vigorous approach to developing new investments, and will operate a 'hands-on' mode of aftercare. These funds include ECI (Equity Capital for Industry), APA (Alan Patricof Associates) and Advent Technology.

Most high-tech venture capital funds do not invest at the pure research phase of a new product or process. It is more usual for them to fund the development or application phase. However, a few high-tech funds do invest at the concept or research phase, notably Prutec, Cogent and Biotechnology Investments.

Universities and high-tech ventures

An important ingredient of this recent trend is the awakening of university departments to the commercialisation possibilities of their research activities. Their awareness has led a number of science-based universities to establish in-house companies to license out their pure science concepts to businesses, which apply these concepts in commercial development. A variation on this theme is the establishment of science parks, linked to universities, which allow companies siting themselves on the science park access to university departments in the technologies where there is a mutual interest. Often the science park has its own venture capital management team, such as Aston University's Birmingham Technology company.

Perhaps the most notable combination of academics and venture capitalists is the formation of Advent Technology, where the venture capital fund's investors include Oxford and Cambridge Universities – which also have a close relationship through their science faculties to those areas of technology where Advent's investment strategy is focused.

Sector specialisation

Venture capital funds that concentrate on high tech usually limit their perspective to relatively few specific sectors. None tries to cover all areas of new technology, while some concentrate on one area only, such as biotechnology (N. M. Rothschild's Biotechnology Investments). How these funds cover each area will vary. Some, such as 3i Ventures, MTI and Prutec, believe that the only viable route is to have a staff of technological specialists who must keep up with developments in the specific industries from which they were recruited into the venture capital industry.

Others, such as Advent and APA, follow the US pattern of a senior full-time staff of experienced venture capitalists with industrial experience. They will have close and regular access to a panel of technical or scientific advisers from the universities, research institutes, and possibly also the R & D departments of companies in the target industries.

A fundamental problem with in-house technological expertise is the ability of the team to keep up with developments in the industry/ technology from which they originate. Product life cycles are ever-shortening in the modern technologies, and research-orientated breakthroughs into new methods are occurring with greater frequency.

The most popular sectors for technological specialisation are probably information technology, telecommunications, medicare (including biotechnology, hardware and clinics), defence and aerospace systems/components, and industrial automation (including computer process control, robotry and instrumentation). Many high-tech funds will concentrate on particular segments rather than on the entire technology sector, and then on a limited number of segments only – typically six or fewer. The reason is practical: the impossibility, economically, of keeping up with the rapid pace of development in more than a few specialist segments.

Feeder funds

A variation on the theme of in-house venture capitalists plus external scientific and technical advisers is the US practice of 'feeder' or affiliated funds. Here, one or a number of venture capital funds 'sponsor' a team of two or three experienced executive-entrepreneurs from a high-tech industry sector, who form an independent specialist management company – the feeder fund. The up-front investment is relatively modest; the objective is for the specialist team to create a flow of investment propositions in their expert area of technology in return for an equity stake in the feeder fund and options into the equity of individual projects. The feeder fund will then finance each deal by leading a syndicate of its own investors – which can include other venture capitalists. Technical evaluation and investment aftercare are provided by the feeder fund's management team.

The feeder fund approach can be used where the sponsoring funds are not themselves focusing on a limited number of high-tech sectors, and where they have a broad spread of investments but also wish to invest in advanced technologies or other specialist forms of venture capital. Feeder funds are still rare in the United Kingdom but include Candover, a management buy-out specialist fund owned by a number of other venture capital funds, Leisure Development, a leisure sector specialist fund owned by five venture capital funds, and Agricultural Technology, a plant biotechnology feeder fund.

Corporate high-tech intrepreneurs

The practice of in-house venture capital activity by large, often technology-based corporations was referred to in Chapter 2. Frequently the prime motive is to obtain a window on their own technology – in order to remain aware of competitive threats and to spot development opportunities – by investing in minority holdings in small businesses within, or peripheral to, their own areas of technology.

This 'intrepreneurship' is rare in Europe but is frequently found in the United States: Monsanto, General Electric, 3M, Du Pont and Exxon are all well known as active participants in the North American venture capital industry. Such major corporations often have highly autonomous in-house units to carry out *directly* venture capital activities of this type, hence the *in*trepreneurs, rather than *en*trepreneurs. Others are persuaded that, to be fully effective, this activity should be carried out *indirectly* by independent venture capital groups whose funding is often provided wholly, or in large part, by the major corporation.

An unusual instance of *indirect intrepreneurship* in Europe is the initiative of Monsanto, which provides half the backing of Advent's £10 million Eurofund – the other half largely deriving from universities and some savings institutions. Another example is Olivetti, the Italian office equipment manufacturer, which has established a *direct*, in-house unit reporting to the Group Chief Executive. This unit takes usually minority investments in small to medium North American high-tech businesses; some of these have eventually become Olivetti subsidiaries.

Risks and rewards

Early-stage high-tech venture capital investment is clearly the most risky of all, with extreme uncertainty regarding product effectiveness and market potential added to the usual financial risk attached to minority equity investment in early-stage businesses. Most 'big winners', however, will develop from this hazardous area, rather than from the more general spread of later-stage venture capital situations. Companies such as Apple, Tandem, Compaq, Oxford Instruments, Rodime, Logica, Federal Express and DPCE are well known on either or both sides of the Atlantic as among the venture capital-backed high-tech big winners of the past few years.

High-tech venture capital investment, apart from high risks, also involves the venture capitalist in a high degree of 'hands-on' management in guiding the entrepreneur through the early years of extreme danger and helping maximise the potential of the later years prior to listing. High-tech investment is not for those venture capital funds that prefer a more passive or reactive 'hands-off' post-investment stance. Some further comments on high-tech funds and on the 'hands-on' style of aftercare will be found in Chapter 13.

Timescale to realisation

It may appear somewhat rigorous to identify different types of funds by their realisation timescales, but there are significant variations. The expectations of many funds and their investors are shorter-term than genuine venture capital allows. Other funds have little need for, or motivations to achieve, realisations.

Capital realisation is the essence of venture capital – to recycle funds for new investments, to demonstrate performance to the fund's investors (in preparation for the next fund launch) and to achieve the fund management's own incentives. Even where a fund is 'open-ended', such as most bank-sponsored captive funds, and there is thus no need for realisations to make new investments, it is a natural motivation in professional venture capitalists to achieve successful realisations.

Funds investing at the *early-stage* financings are inevitably taking a medium- to long-term (5–7 years) view of their eventual pay-back or realisation. The majority of projects or businesses they are backing will require such a timescale to achieve an adequate growth record to tempt either a trade buyer or stock market (or USM/OTC) investors.

Some early-stage venture capitalists, indeed, adopt a very long-term view, notably those few funds in pre-start-up high-technology project financings – where ten years or so is regarded as a tolerable timescale to pay-back. This kind of timescale is rare in the United Kingdom, but must be expected by entrants into the fields of biotechnology, intelligent computer systems and satellite communications. It may also apply (despite optimistic promoters) to cable TV, optic fibre telecoms and cellular radio systems.

Development capitalists, engaged in later-stage financings, are usually investing in mature, proven businesses with real prospects of some form of (stock) market quotation three years or so from investment, provided the entrepreneur is seeking a realisation – not always the case with development capital.

Later-stage financings often provide a satisfactory running yield for their investors, permitting the funds involved to take a relaxed view if their investment fails to realise in a 3–5 year timescale. Such a relaxed view may mean that realisations become rare while the satisfactory yield is maintained. The overall fund performance, including capital growth, can thus fall below that of the incomeless early-stage specialist, who can only be judged by capital growth performance.

Among the many recent entrants into the UK venture capital industry are those tempted by the apparent ease of early realisations, due to the availability of the Unlisted Securities Market and various over-the-counter markets. Such potentially short-term horizons in what is essentially a long-term business may lead to excessive expectations of a rapid flow of highly profitable realisations. Venture capital funds with these ambitions may have neither the skilled manpower resources necessary nor the stamina for what is likely to be a longer haul. A further danger is that they may neglect to set aside adequate spare liquidity for the follow-on finance which often will be necessary for existing investments before successful realisations can be made.

Realisations may not be of prime importance in the objectives of *State-owned* or State-related funds. The main objective is usually to create or preserve employment with an open-ended source of funds from the State, thus involving no need to recycle investments.

For an entrepreneur seeking venture capital, it is critically important to establish the realisation horizons of his potential backers in order to avoid painful disagreements and disappointment at a later stage – when he may find his backers wanting to realise their investment before he is ready, or the reverse. Divorce in venture capital is much more difficult and costly than in the domestic equivalent.

Geographical limitation

UK internally

Before the 1980s few funds were regionally specialised. Notable exceptions were the four major State financing organisations: the Scottish Development Agency, Welsh Development Agency, Northern Ireland Development Agency and National Enterprise Board – which had all of England as its region. Since then, most of the State-related funds which have been established are regionally based to some extent and invest only in their designated areas. Examples are the West Midlands Enterprise Board, Greater Manchester Enterprise Board, Merseyside Enterprise Fund and Western Enterprise Fund (Devon and Cornwall).

A number of institution-backed funds have also been established with regional briefs. These include Rainford Venture Capital (Lancashire and Merseyside), Anglo-American Ventures (Northern England), Avon Enterprise Fund (Gloucestershire, Somerset, Avon and Wiltshire) and Darnaway (Scotland). SUMIT (Sharp Unquoted Midlands Investment Trust) began with a regional brief but has investments in other parts of England as well. A similar national development from a regional base has been carried out by Melville Street Investments from its Scottish origins.

The Business Expansion Scheme has brought a new regional emphasis to venture capital in that many BES funds operate within a specifically defined geographical area. Some of these are Mercia (West Midlands), Northern Capital Ventures (Scotland and Northern England), The Yorkshire Capital Ventures Fund, Centreway (Midlands), Oak (Manchester, Cheshire and Lancashire) and Sapling (Lancashire).

In many cases it is worth while for an entrepreneur seeking venture capital to approach funds operating within his region as well as those operating nationally. Some regional funds, however, have relatively limited sums available and can thus accommodate only the smaller propositions (say under £200,000) without recourse to syndication, often with a national fund or funds.

UK externally

By far the majority of UK venture capital funds operate exclusively in the United Kingdom and do not make investments overseas. Exceptions are 3i Ventures, which has venture capital operations or associates in the United States, France and the Netherlands; Charterhouse Development (USA, France and Canada); CIN Industrial Investments (USA); Abingworth (USA); APA (France and USA); Advent (Belgium, West Germany, Singapore and USA); Newmarket (USA); and Murray Technology and Murray Electronics (USA). ECI has also recently established links with venture capital funds on the east and west coasts of the United States and with funds in the Netherlands, France, Belgium and West Germany.

Undoubtedly, such links will grow, particularly as the world's high-technology markets become truly international, with intense competition above all from North America and the Far East.

Even if most UK-based venture capital funds do not at present invest directly abroad, many will finance the overseas expansion plans (including acquisitions) of UK-based companies. Many will also finance UK projects of overseas-owned companies on a joint-venture basis.

Part two The venture capital spectrum

Introduction

The course of business growth cannot be described in a strictly com-
partmentalised way. There are, however, identifiable stages in corporate development, each of which has distinct characteristics,
although the stages merge in the continuous process of growth.

The venture capital industry recognises these different stages to the
extent that most funds specialise in one or more (but rarely all). These
specialisms, as outlined in Table 5, are as follows:

(a) *early-stage financings*:
   – seed capital (pre-start-up/R & D project finance);
   – start-ups;
   – second-round finance, for young companies;
(b) *later-stage financings*, or development capital, for established
   businesses:
   – expansion finance;
   – replacement capital;
   – turnarounds;
   – buy-outs.

The early stages of seed capital, start-ups and second-round finance are
described in Chapter 4. The later stages are covered in Chapters 5
and 6.

Not all businesses pass through each of the stages in a sequential
manner. In particular, *seed capital* is not normally required by service-
based businesses involved in retail, wholesale or catering activities.
While a restaurant or video film distributor may require start-up
finance, it is difficult to see how seed capital could be required unless the
restaurateur wished first to grow his own vegetables or the video
distributor to make his own films. Seed capital applies largely to manu-

Table 5. A venture capital spectrum

	Timescale (years)	Risk
Early-stage investment		
Seed capital	7–10	Extreme
Prototype development		
Start-up	5–10	Very high
Business launch		
Second-round	3–7	High
Trading, but loss-making or just profitable		
Later-stage investment		
Mezzanine/development capital	1–3	Medium
Established and profitable; needs expansion finance		
Bridge	1–3	Low
Last round before planned exit		
Buy-out	1–3	Low
All stages		
Turnaround	3–5	Medium to high
New management and rescue finance		

facturing and research-based service activities – such as software houses or specialised information services.

Similarly, *second-round finance* does not always follow *start-up capital*. If the business grows successfully, it may generate sufficient cash to fund its own growth until much later – possibly until it is quoted on the stock market.

Early-stage finance, whether seed, start-up or second-round, is where the debt versus equity debate is most relevant. For a young, growing company which has not yet reached profitability to finance its early stages through borrowings, rather than equity-type risk capital, can seriously damage the health of the business. Chapter 12 deals with this fundamental issue in venture capital.

Early-stage finance is also where the venture capitalist has to adopt a 'hands-on' approach to his investments. It is rarely sufficient, in providing equity risk capital for businesses at the 'seed', start-up or even second-round stage, to provide the money and walk away – relying on semi-annual and annual financial reporting. Both to protect the investment from failure and to enhance its progress, the venture capitalist will play an active partner's supporting role to the entrepreneur's 'lead'. On occasion, the venture capitalist may have to take over as general business manager, with the entrepreneur concentrating on technical, production or marketing matters.

Many venture capital funds choose not to – or are not equipped to – play a 'hands-on' role, and thus will tend to exclude themselves from early-stage financings. The workload in a 'hands-on' fund involves a higher staff-to-investment ratio than is required with later-stage financings. It also involves a high content of industrially experienced managers in the fund's staffing.

In later-stage financings, wherever business management gaps appear, it is usual for the venture capitalist to persuade the entrepreneur to recruit externally rather than have the fund itself provide the 'hands-on' expertise.

Overall, some 20% of venture capital-backed companies reach the public share markets, 40% are merged into larger firms, 20% fail and 20% continue to exist but do not achieve their investors' expectations. The ratio of failure rises to 40% in early-stage projects.

4 Early-stage financing

Seed capital/R & D projects

Before a product-based business can be established, there is often a lengthy process of research and development (R & D), starting with the initial concept. This concept will form the basis of a research project which may then proceed to the development phase prior to commercial application in the form of a corporate entity – usually a limited company. The initial concept may arise from the investor's own experience or research work, from that of academic institutions or from technology transfer – possibly through licensing. The last process is more common in the development or commercialisation phase than in the research phase.

For small businesses, initial financial requirements are usually modest in the research phase, and often the inventor/entrepreneur finds sufficient from his own resources: savings, second mortgage, family funds and friends' loans. This is the stage of extreme improbability *vis-à-vis* the eventual emergence of a viable enterprise.

The financial risks mount progressively as the research phase moves into the development phase, where a prototype product is tested prior to commercialisation. It is during this phase that external finance is often sought by the inventor/entrepreneur as his own capital is consumed. Figure 1 portrays the typical S-curve in a new technology product or process launch.

The essence of successful project application in this phase is to match the entrepreneur's technical or product knowledge to a market opportunity. The key financial risk is the marketing risk. The investment in developing the technology is usually dwarfed by that required to market the product, process or service. The quality of marketing management

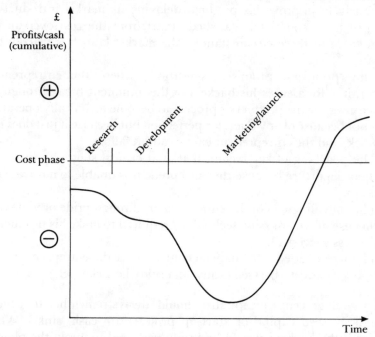

Fig. 1 The technology S-curve

becomes crucial at this stage – a factor often not recognised, or not accepted, by the entrepreneur and his backers.

The commercial awareness of the inventor is absolutely vital to the success of a seed capital or start-up project. If the inventor already has or can develop this commercialism, he may become a successful entrepreneur. Without it, he and his project are likely to partner each other into failure.

Among the traps for both entrepreneur and venture capitalist at the seed capital stage are the following:

(a) The increasing compression of product life cycles in most modern technologies;
(b) A lack of awareness of international competition.
(c) The failure to gain adequate patent protection, or where this is not possible the inability to get the product, process or service successfully launched ahead of the competition.
(d) Being too early into the market, before potential consumers are ready for the product, process or service.
(e) The 'perfection syndrome', whereby the entrepreneur seeks contin-

uously to improve his product, delaying its market introduction until he is completely satisfied; apart from the cost overrun inevitable in these circumstances, the market launch is usually too late.

(f) The 'promises, promises' syndrome, where the entrepreneur continually assures his backers of the imminent breakthrough he requires for the product or process to become technically operative – not because of any quest for perfection but because it just does not work, and the entrepreneur cannot admit failure.

(g) The poaching of key technical staff at critical stages by rivals, or their departure because the entrepreneur is unable to motivate his team.

(h) The unwillingness of the entrepreneur, through pride or vanity, to 'license in' any missing technology required to make his product or process successful.

(i) The lack of adequate financial controls over the entrepreneur who may be gadget-obsessed or just an untidy housekeeper.

An early-stage venture capitalist should always remember that high-technology seed capital or start-up projects are cash 'sinks'. When required, the backers should be firmly prepared to apply the plug to halt the drainage.

The financial partner should provide, at least in his own mind, for a doubling or trebling of his initial commitment. Further tranches of finance can take the form of an increased equity share, unsecured loans, or a combination of the two.

Another aspect of UK early-stage, high-technology projects is that of limited market size in the United Kingdom and Europe. To be successful on the scale required to achieve 'big winners', a larger market potential must be available, particularly that of the United States. The risks are as great with UK as with US high-tech projects but the rewards substantially less if the European markets alone are tackled. The risks of setting up in the United States are considerable for a small UK business, and thus the whole area of outward technology transfer is particularly relevant to a UK high-tech entrepreneur and his venture capitalists.

It was natural in the past for local clearing-bank branches to be the first source of external seed capital through overdrafts covered by the entrepreneur's personal guarantee. Note that this is not equity or permanent capital, but short-term borrowing which can be recalled on demand.

In the past decade, however, the inclination of venture capitalists to provide equity-type seed capital has increased, although only to a limited extent. There are at present probably no more than a handful of venture capital funds prepared to provide regular amounts of seed or pre-start-up capital (e.g. 3i Ventures, Prutec, Cogent, Innotech and NRDC). In its first year, the Business Start-up Scheme appeared as if it would provide some seed capital as well as filling the equity gap for smaller-scale start-ups. The rapid supplanting of the BSS by the Business Expansion Scheme, favouring the more established and mature business, has meant that seed capital is most unlikely to be available from that source.

Industrial joint ventures are another possibility for entrepreneurs seeking seed capital. This usually means, however, that the entrepreneur surrenders the opportunity of developing his own business. The industrial partner normally seeks control over the R & D project and negotiates pre-emptive rights over future marketing and licensing in return for a royalty fee.

One area of possible hope for the entrepreneur seeking seed capital may be the university-linked science parks. At present in their infancy, they have – in the United States – assisted seed capital projects with both expertise and financing in return for a share in the project's equity and a commitment by the entrepreneur, if successful, to establish his business on the science park.

There are a number of venture capital funds which invest in R & D projects as part of their overall activity. Typically, these are well-established 'general' funds with a spread of investments but some appetite for early-stage financings (seed and start-up projects) as a higher-risk or 'speculative' activity for a part of their portfolio. Among such funds are Equity Capital for Industry, Electra, Advent, APA, Citicorp Venture Capital, MTI and the Murray Johnstone investment trusts.

Evaluation of seed capital projects is hazardous, and here the venture capitalist's instinctive judgement is called to the fore. Often the project will not result in a working model, let alone a commercial prototype. There may not be an adequate market for the product/service, or others may get there first. The entrepreneur may be overtaken by technology, or may not be able to produce at a user-acceptable price. Genuine evidence for the project's potential may not exist.

The seed capital venture fund will look for evidence of a successful performance record in the inventor/entrepreneur's previous experience of similar products, technology and markets. He will have to demonstrate qualities of business management as well as technical innovation. He will also have to produce a realistic business plan, albeit founded inevitably on a matrix of guesses about the future for his project.

Once it gains access to equity from a venture capital source, a seed or pre-start-up R & D project is not easy to structure financially. There are rarely any assets, by definition no income, a stream of costs whose magnitude is uncertain and a timescale of one-way stretching elasticity. It is probable that the estimated costs and timescale until start-up or commercialisation will at least double or triple, and allowance should be made for this in the financing structure.

Annexe 1A (page 176) illustrates a typical seed capital investment and alternative financing structures.

Start-ups

The start-up is widely regarded as the essence of venture capital activity, so much so that many people use the terms 'start-up' and 'venture capital' interchangeably. Perhaps the most exciting and risky aspect of venture capital is the launch of a new business, often after a period of R & D. At the start-up stage the entrepreneur and his product or service are as yet untried, the finance required usually dwarfs his own resources, and the problems he has to overcome to realise even a modest success are manifold.

Not all start-ups are of the first-time inventor or 'greenfield' variety, so beloved of transatlantic venture capital myth. Many new enterprises are formed by experienced people wishing to launch their own business in an industry they know well. Others are spin-offs from research bodies or large corporations, where a venture capitalist joins with an industrially experienced or corporate partner.

Still other start-ups occur where an existing, generally smaller, company wishes to license new technology from a research source or overseas-based business and does not have adequate financial resources. In this case a venture capitalist may invest directly in the established company, in a subsidiary constructed to effect the start-up or in a joint venture. If either of the last two paths is followed, it is customary for the venture capitalist to require some protective rights through, for example, conversion into the parent company's shares. This type of start-up is the least risky and is more like later-stage finance.

At present, more venture capital funds are prepared to provide equity finance for start-ups than for seed capital projects. Most funds, however, prefer second- or later-stage equity financings, and no UK fund invests solely in 'greenfield' start-ups. Among the relatively few funds investing in start-ups are Prutec, 3i Ventures, Innotech, Baronsmead, Advent, Equity Capital for Industry, Alan Patricof Associates, Midland Bank Venture Capital, MTI (Managed Technology Investments) and Thompson Clive.

With a start-up (unlike R & D projects) there is, or should be, some indication of the potential market for the product or service which forms the basis of the new business. There is also a formal structure, usually a limited company, and at least the rudiments of an organisation; i.e. the entrepreneur is no longer the sole manager, although his team may be a very small one.

A professional venture capitalist will pay more than standard attention to the entrepreneur's business plan in a start-up. His market size, growth and market share assumptions will be thoroughly investigated, both by the venture capitalist's own team and possibly by outside specialists – particularly if a new technology or market is involved. The entrepreneur's management team will come under severe scrutiny for balanced skills, personal 'fit' and financial commitment.

A start-up deal structure is the result of a particularly acute bargaining process for the entrepreneur who wants to retain control over his new business but has already exhausted his own resources. On the other side is the venture capitalist, who is asked to provide 90% or more of the finance required and consequently seeks a fair share of the equity, which is the basis of his eventual reward – a capital gain on realisation through a stock market, USM or OTC listing, or a trade sale.

Historically, there has been extreme reluctance on the part of entrepreneurs in the United Kingdom to surrender equity at the start-up stage. Although there are signs of a change in this peculiarly European attitude, most start-up finance is still provided through loans of various kinds.

Loan finance is now available on unusually advantageous terms (no personal guarantee, no security) through the Government's Loan Guarantee Scheme (LGS) in amounts up to £75,000. Some £500 million has already been drawn under the LGS.

There are some fundamental and frequently irreconcilable problems in financing start-ups relating to the venture capitalist's favoured debt equity/structure, and to the onerous requirement by certain providers of start-up capital for an income yield from the outset. The debt versus equity issue is discussed in Chapter 12, together with other key issues concerning the future of venture capital in the United Kingdom.

Start-ups are undoubtedly the most fertile source of the 'big winners' of which all venture capitalists dream. This area is also a graveyard of failed projects. The risks are probably higher with start-ups than with seed capital projects, largely because the amounts invested are substantially greater. Start-ups are the most demanding of a venture capitalist's skill, involving continuous management effort. Before a start-up can reach fruition through a satisfactory realisation, the original backers will likely have to follow their first-round investment with subsequent financings several times the size of their initial commitment.

When the start-up entrepreneur is choosing his backer, he will be wise to select a team with start-up experience and an availability of follow-up finance. He will also seek their agreement in principle to provide further funds at a later stage.

A feature of many start-ups is the need, at some stage, for the venture capitalist to play an active role in strengthening second-line management in the investment. When the business is up and running, weaknesses in key people may become apparent. While the entrepreneur may not fall short in this respect (or the venture capitalist will have made a cardinal error of judgement), his management team may prove to be deficient in certain skills. Often the entrepreneur will not have hired senior management before. It is therefore critical to the success of the business and the investment that entrepreneur and venture capitalist are at one in identifying such deficiencies, in deciding how to remedy them, and finally in agreeing on whom to appoint.

By contrast, in later-stage venture capital activity the management team is likely to be many-layered, and it is frequently possible for senior management to appoint staff from within to fill gaps, or at least to recruit externally without recourse to the venture capital backers. Moreover, in more established businesses any single management appointment is likely to be far less critical than it would be during a start-up.

On the whole, start-ups require from their backers stronger stomachs than do the other stages of venture capital, as well as a retention of part of the fund for follow-up or second-round investment and a longer timescale to realisation. The greatest venture capital legends, as well as the significantly more numerous disasters, stem from this stage of corporate development.

Statistics on the success ratio of UK start-ups are not currently available in a reliable form. (According to one long-established source, between one-third and one half of all start-ups fail within the first two years.) In the United States, the conventional wisdom (based on fact) is that for every ten start-ups, two fail in the first two or three years and two stagger on through to year five and then expire – making four failures. Of the remaining six, one will become a big winner, one a moderate winner and the other four will survive in some form of inadequate gain, in a quaintly named transatlantic category of 'the living dead'.

Annexe 1B (page 178) illustrates three forms of start-up deal structure from a variety of possible alternatives.

Second-round finance

There are positive and negative reasons why early stages of development may require further funding after start-up but before the business is established.

Among the negative reasons is that there is often a period of loss after start-up, during which the start-up capital is consumed and debt incurred which outgrows the equity base of the business. Entrepreneur and venture capitalist alike then have a tough decision to make: continue, or call it a day and go into receivership or liquidation.

To continue inevitably requires a second tranche of equity-type funding, which in most cases has to be provided by the original backers. The business has not yet established a profitable performance record, and the entrepreneur is unlikely to attract new investors as partners for the start-up venture capitalist.

In such a position, the entrepreneur will probably have to accept a reduction in his own stake since his backers will require a proper equity reward for the increased amount they will have at risk. The venture capitalist is also likely to exert closer control over the way in which the second tranche of equity is spent. On occasion, the venture capitalist and/or the entrepreneur may have to guarantee further bank borrowings by the company as well.

Among the positive reasons for second-round finance is that the business may be growing at such a rate (or have such clear potential) that even where only small profits – if any – are being achieved, new investors can be attracted to provide this first stage of expansion finance after start-up.

Depending on the relationship at the time between the entrepreneur and his venture capitalists, it may be that his original backers will provide the entire second-round financing. However, there are circumstances where new investors are necessary:

(a) The size of second-round finance needed may be beyond the investment limits of the existing investors, even though they may be enthusiastic about the business.

(b) The original investors may already have a large share of the company's equity and may not be willing to increase this share, which in certain circumstances might give them control; they may even have lost some or all confidence in the entrepreneur.

(c) The entrepreneur may not wish the existing investors to have a larger holding; indeed, he may have lost confidence in them.

(d) The entrepreneur may wish to broaden his investor base prior to a stock market listing for his business.

(e) The further development of the company may require access to specialist technical skills or market contacts which can be supplied only by a new investor.

(f) The original investors may have run out of money or may no longer exist; they may have been taken over by another organisation with different objectives; or they may have failed to survive in the increasingly tough and competitive world of venture capital.

Second-round financing attracts more venture capitalists than either R & D projects or start-ups. However, it is not of universal appeal, with a large number of funds limiting their activities to later-stage financings.

The structuring of second-round financing can be quite complex, particularly when new investors are involved. There is often extensive bargaining over the price of entry, the degree of 'hands-on' involvement they seek and their relationship with the original investors.

Second-round investment may be made with the same financial instrument(s) used for the start-up; usually, however, it takes a different form tailored to the forward requirements of the business and will often incorporate, for the first time, an income yield to the investor.

Annexe 1C (page 180) illustrates two alternative structures for second-round financing from among the many possible variations.

5 Later-stage financing

Most of the funds active in the pre-1980 era of UK venture capital concentrated their energies on development capital or *later-stage* financing. In the United States a new phrase has been coined for this activity: mezzanine finance. In essence, we are talking about funding established businesses, which have passed through the hazards of *early-stage* financing. These businesses may be mature (i.e. not high-growth) but can still have attractive yield and capital growth prospects. They usually have at least a five-year record of profits, an identifiable market position and a formal organisation structure – with one or more layers of management below the entrepreneur's top team. Such businesses are generally more stable, and thus lower-risk, than the typical early-stage business. Exceptions are *turnaround* or recovery situations, where the venture capitalist has to accept a significantly higher degree of risk; these are rare in the United Kingdom due largely to investor reluctance. Other recognisable types of development capital are *expansion finance*, *replacement capital* (or 'money out' for the entre-preneur) and *buy-outs*, of which there are three main forms: *management*, *receivership* and *share repurchase*.

In today's venture capital industry the majority of funds, including many Business Expansion Scheme funds, strongly prefer later-stage investment to the early-stage seed capital projects and start-ups. Indeed, several funds have development capital in their titles, e.g. Charterhouse Development Capital, Fountain Development Fund and Development Capital Limited. Some specialise in buy-outs, but few are prepared to invest in turnarounds. All are prepared to finance expansion projects, and most (except BES funds) will provide replace-ment capital for an entrepreneur seeking some 'money out', i.e. the realisation of part of his shareholding – whether or not this is prior to a listing or subsequent trade sale.

A characteristic of most funds active in development capital, BES funds excepted, is their requirement for income (a running yield). There is, of course, a keen interest in achieving an eventual capital gain; the fund usually seeks a balance between income now and capital profits later. Clearly, at this stage, most companies can afford to satisfy their investors' income requirements.

The company is probably generating after-tax profits adequate for both retentions and dividends to the investor. The entrepreneur is usually not interested in receiving dividends himself because of his own income tax position. It is common, therefore, to arrive at a formula that gives the investing fund a dividend based on an agreed proportion of available profits, taking into account corporation tax.

It is rare for an investing fund to have a majority equity position in an expansion finance or replacement capital investment. In larger turn-arounds and buy-outs, however, it is often the case – because of the substantial amounts of finance required in relation to the resources of the manager-shareholders – that the incoming funds will together have a majority or controlling position.

Even where the development capitalist has a minority position, he will rarely depart from a negotiated right to approve major capital expenditure items, acquisitions or disposals, and key management appointments. He will usually appoint a nominated non-executive director to the board of the investee company; this director will frequently, but not always, be the leader of the team who investigated and negotiated the investment. The development capitalist will also expect a formal procedure concerning regular board meetings, effective management controls, and a flow of monitoring information from the company.

In the past, the most common form of exit from a development capital investment, for both entrepreneur and investors, was a trade sale. Since the advent of the Unlisted Securities Market it is now at least as likely that the exit will be through a USM listing, or possibly a full quote.

Chapter 6 is concerned entirely with *buy-outs*, an important and relatively new aspect of later-stage finance which, at present, probably accounts for more than a third of all development capital investments. This chapter concentrates on *expansion finance, replacement capital* and *turnarounds*, the other most readily identifiable forms of later-stage finance.

Expansion finance

This self-descriptive phrase embraces two basic paths of development for an established business: organic growth or growth by acquisition. There are many books on the theory and practice of growth, and many more on acquisition strategy, tactics and experience. As far as the venture capitalist is concerned, there is little distinction between the two kinds of growth when assessing their relative attractions. Organic expansion implies new or larger factories/warehouses, new products, new markets and overseas development. Acquisition may accomplish similar aims through the purchase of an existing business, or simply of business assets.

In either case the investing fund(s) will require a well-founded business plan, both for existing activities and for those to be developed. Where an acquisition is involved, the investor will need to meet the vendors and carry out his own appraisal of the 'beneficial fit' with the purchaser – his potential investee company.

In many cases the purchaser will be an existing investee company which the investing fund knows well, but there will be transactions where the investor knows neither the purchasing business nor the business to be acquired. On these occasions the investigation/negotiation process may be extended since three principals are involved (investor, vendor and purchaser), none of whom has established a record or position of trust with the others.

There are also acquisition-financing investments where the venture capitalist has already invested in the business being sold. He may be asked by the purchaser to help finance the acquisition of this business. He may even be instrumental in bringing about the acquisition if he is dissatisfied with the progress of his investment and thus seeks a purchaser as an alternative either to putting more at risk in the same business or to receivership/liquidation of his investment.

The deal structure suitable to an expansion finance investment, whether organic or acquisition-based, is almost infinitely variable. It will depend upon the debt structure of both businesses, the potential long-term benefits of the merger and the maximum equity dilution acceptable to the purchaser in whose business the venture capitalist will invest.

Annexe 2A (page 182) illustrates two typical expansion financing deal structures from ECI's own experience; there are many possible variations on these examples.

Replacement capital

Much of the past investment by development capital funds has been through 'money out' or replacement capital deals. Certain funds, including Charterhouse Development, Midland Bank Industrial Finance and EDITH (Estate Duties Investment Trust, ICFC's sister company in the 3i Group), made up to half of their investments by purchasing existing shares from entrepreneurs or their families, to give the funds minority holdings.

Frequently, the entrepreneur does not plan a stock market listing in the near future; hence the fund's requirement for a reasonable income yield in lieu of a foreseeable capital profit. Capital profits can, of course, materialise, whether through a quotation on The Stock Exchange or a trade sale. However, such profits have been seen as 'the cream on the coffee', an adequate running yield being 'the coffee'.

The vendor of shares to the fund has not always been the entrepreneur or members of his management team. In mature private or public companies, there is often a wide spread of shareholdings resulting from inheritance and trust dispersals over the years. The non-involved members of a family company often meet demands for immediate cash through a sale of shares. Another cause of 'money out' deals may be a rift within a family grouping or a quarrel between two or more founder-partners.

Although the fund's initial holding may be simply a purchase of shares, which does not itself provide finance for the company, there may be possibilities for further funding of a 'money in' nature to assist the company's expansion. Thus an entrepreneur contemplating the sale of shares to an investing fund should always assess the ability and willingness of the fund to provide further finance. Indeed, the investing fund may agree to some forward commitment of this kind, providing a drawdown facility of loan stock and even preference shares or other equity-type capital.

The structuring of a replacement capital deal is relatively straightforward if the company is to remain unlisted. It is usual for the fund to buy ordinary shares from the vendor(s) and then convert these into a preferred instrument bearing a fixed dividend coupon. Such an instrument may be preferred ordinary or preference shares. The shares will often be convertible back into ordinary shares if the company is listed or sold; they may participate in profits growth through participating in profits above a certain threshold, to give an additional income yield.

With the arrival of the Granville & Co. (formerly M. J. H. Nightingale) over-the-counter market in the early 1970s, the launch of The Stock Exchange's own Unlisted Securities Market in 1980 and the recent arrival of a second OTC market on the fringes of the stock market, the entrepreneur and his family are now spoilt for choice if they wish to realise part of their shareholdings.

It is not, therefore, surprising that the flow of 'money out' deals to venture capital funds active in replacement capital has lessened since 1980. However, there are still entrepreneurs who have no wish to be quoted on the OTC, USM or Stock Exchange for reasons related to freedom of action, privacy and antipathy to the short-term performance spotlight that is inherent in the USM and Stock Exchange.

In addition, it is quite common for an entrepreneur to seek a partial realisation on the way to some form of quotation, either because he has personal debts arising from his start-up phase or because he wishes to enjoy some of the fruits of his labours while continuing to build the company towards a larger realisation at a later date. Such deals can be readily financed, provided the entrepreneur is genuine in his motivation and is not seeking to get out while he can – his business having already passed its peak performance, with little or no chance of a future OTC, USM or stock market listing.

Business Expansion Scheme funds are not used for 'money out' deals as they can participate only in the issue of new shares by a company for expansion projects or similar purposes.

Annexe 2B (page 184) illustrates a typical 'money out' deal structure.

Turnarounds

The American phrase 'turnarounds' is often translated in the United Kingdom as 'recovery situations'. It is a rare form of later-stage finance in which few funds are prepared to invest. Among those that do are Equity Capital for Industry, 3i (ICFC), CIN Industrial Investments (the National Coal Board Pension Fund) and Electra Investment Trust. BES funds are not yet evident in the turnaround/recovery arena.

A recovery situation in an unquoted company can occur during the early stages of development if the entrepreneur has failed to control his cash flow or has acquired too great a burden of debt rather than equity (see Chapter 12). His launch programmme may have been too ambitious and costly, the market may be slow to realise the potential of his product or service, or it may turn out that he lacks some key management skills although he is an able inventor or technologist. In early-stage turnarounds it is almost always the original backers who have to carry out the recovery. New investors are unlikely to be attracted at this stage.

Recovery situations at the later stages of development occur most often where there is no outside or professional investor involved. If there were original venture capital backers, they would already have sorted out the problems or perhaps not have allowed them to occur in the first place. The investment may also have been lost through receivership or liquidation, in which case, of course, there is no prospect of recovery – although there may well be the opportunity for a receivership buy-out (see Chapter 6). There are instances, however, of an original investor either not having the staff necessary to tackle a problem investment or not being too concerned about its future. He may already have tried and failed; or perhaps the investment represents a relatively small risk in his total portfolio.

Whether or not the company in difficulty has an investor, a turn-around or recovery case requires specialist skill. It will probably mean a vigorous renegotiation of the company's borrowing facilities with its bankers, possibly including a creditor's moratorium. Above all, it means management changes. These may require the original entrepreneur to step aside to an advisory role or to leave the company altogether. Further, in most recovery situations a substantial investment will be required, which may give majority control to the venture capitalist.

'Hands-on' venture capital management is required with turn-arounds. The venture capitalist will, either working alone or together with an externally appointed executive chairman, play an active day-to-day role in management decisions throughout the crisis period, which can last anywhere from six months to two years.

When confronted by a potential recovery situation, the venture capitalist must decide quickly whether the business has genuine prospects, not simply of returning to health, but also of sustaining profitable growth thereafter. There is no sense in a risk/reward ratio which results from investing in a company that can limp back to survival as one of the 'walking wounded' (UK style) or 'living dead' (US style) but has no better prospects.

It is rare, in recovery situations, to find the same 'big winners' as in early-stage investments that develop rapidly towards a listing. In many cases, the turnaround company will be a mature business in a traditional industry. Where the business is in a modern sector of industry, it may have lost a market or technological lead and cannot completely fulfil its original growth prospects.

Often, the eventual realisation for a turnaround venture capitalist will be the trade sale to a larger company in the same industry. A moderately good capital profit can thus be made, but usually no more than two to three times the original investment – except in the case of an early-stage high-tech turnaround, where higher profits can be expected.

It should not be forgotten, however, that many recovery situations end in failure despite the efforts of the incoming venture capitalist or, at best, struggle on without reward to the investing fund. It is not difficult to see why so few venture capital funds are prepared to invest in turnaround situations. This is a specialist form of venture capital activity and is, in itself, subject enough for a book.

Annexe 2C (page 185) describes an actual deal structure for a turnaround situation from ECI's own portfolio (including a BES offer).

6 Buy-outs

Growth of buy-outs

The buy-out is a relatively recent form of investment in the European venture capital industry. In essence, it involves the creation of independent businesses by separating them from their existing owners, which may be successful or unsuccessful corporations, or family-controlled businesses. A buy-out will involve the existing or a new management team and a set of assets which may simply be a trade name or a small group of people. In most cases it will also involve one or more new investors, although in some cases buy-outs can be financed from the management team's own resources and/or through bank debt alone.

There have been buy-outs in the United Kingdom on a sporadic basis since the early 1960s; these reached a consistent and high volume only in the early 1980s. The practice has been active in the United States, however, since the early 1950s. The first practitioners of buy-outs in the United Kingdom were not US banks, venture capital funds or institutions with experience of the US market, but rather domestic merchant banks and savings institutions.

As will be seen from Table 6, there was a rapid growth in management buy-outs between 1980 and 1983, resulting largely from the general economic problems experienced by major industrial groupings due to the UK recession and subsequently the world recession. These large groups have found it necessary or desirable to realise cash by disposal of peripheral activities in order to sustain the core of their business and to avoid management stretch into non-essential activities.

The early indications are that 1984 will show a result at around the same level as 1983 of some 200 transactions, involving a total of £150

Table 6. UK buy-out statistics

	1967–76	1977	1978	1979	1980	1981	1982	1983
Conventional acquisitions of which:	6,088	481	567	534	469	452	463	447
Subsidiaries acquired by new parent	1,434	110	125	117	101	121	164	142
Management buy-outs (MBOs)	43	13	23	52	107	124	170	200
MBOs % of subsidiaries acquired	3	12	18	44	106	102	104	141

Source: J. Coyne and M. Wright, Nottingham University.

million. This stabilisation in the volume of buy-outs is at least partially due to recovery by the larger corporations. Another factor is the corporate vendor's increasing awareness of the 'resale' value of the corporation's peripheral businesses. A significant comparative statistic, which highlights the importance of the buy-out trend, is that between 1980 and 1983 there were more buy-outs than acquisitions by other industrial companies of divested subsidiaries. In 1977, by contrast, acquisitions were roughly ten times the number of buy-outs. It should also be noted that buy-outs are currently smaller, at about half the size of subsidiaries sold to new parents.

Indeed, a striking feature has been the small size of most buy-outs, with an average size of under £1 million consideration/valuation and fewer than 200 employees. Many of these small buy-outs are mature businesses which have been in existence for a long time. It is difficult to predict how many will prosper and grow in time to become substantial businesses in their own right and how many will either fail in their now independent position or remain as they were when bought out, i.e. unexciting and without real growth prospects. A number, however, are businesses with real growth potential, often in high-technology areas but distinct from the main activity of their former parent.

It is interesting to note that the largest UK buy-out to date was £54 million for the National Freight Corporation in 1982, which basically involved only the employees and bank debt. Other large buy-outs have been William Timpson (£40m), Paragon (£16.75m), Ansafone (1981 – £13.5m) and Stone International (1982 – £13m).

The major hazard with many buy-outs is the high initial gearing (ratio of debt to equity) inherent in the normal funding structure, particularly where gearing is made up of bank lending rather than long-term preference capital. The use of equity-based syndications helps to keep the initial debt low and thus gives the company essential breathing space in its early years as an independent entity. However, most UK buy-outs include debt as a substantial proportion of the total funding, often where asset disposals can be safely predicted to quickly reduce the initial level of debt. In smaller buy-outs (under £1 million) management teams can often achieve ultimate control of the equity, while typically subscribing only 10–20% of the total funds. In larger buy-outs it is common for the managers to hold only a minority equity position, and gearing is often lower.

Why buy-outs?

There are a number of reasons why the buy-out has become such an important activity in the venture capital market-place.

Creation of smaller-scale enterprise. The buy-out is an additional and perhaps a more certain mechanism for the creation of small and medium-sized businesses, particularly when compared with start-ups of new technology-based firms.

Reversal of three decades of industrial concentration. The process of de-merger and creation of smaller, more flexible profit centres is part of the divestment process of today's large industrial groups. These groups were built up after 1950 by uninterrupted merger and acquisition activity, and have generally shown themselves particularly ill-suited to today's conditions of rapid technological and economic change.

Remarriage of management and ownership. An unfortunate trend in the twentieth century has been the divorce of management of enterprises from their ownership. Efficiency has suffered through successful defence by inadequate management against the best interests of the owners. The buy-out provides the opportunity for common identification of goals by managers and owners, the managers in many cases actually being the owners.

Investor/banker common interest. Apart from the divorce of management and ownership, one of the major weaknesses of twentieth-century economic development has been the separation of interest between banker and investor, with the former concerned largely with security, i.e. the absence of risk. The buy-out, with its usually high initial gearing, often unsecured, provides an opportunity for banker and investor to agree on a common aim from the outset and proceed as partners with the management, throughout the good and bad early years, of their buy-out's development.

Development of new entrepreneurs. After 30 years of growth of the 'organisation man' and the cult of the industrial bureaucrat, the buy-out presents a long-needed injection of new entrepreneurial skill by freeing the corporate manager from his umbilical cord to corporate headquarters. (As we shall see later, however, there are risks involved in this.)

Lower-risk investment than start-ups. Largely because of the established performance record of the business being bought out and of the management effecting the buy-out, and because of the established asset position, a buy-out represents a significantly lower degree of risk, in most cases, than does the new technology start-up. It should be noted, however, that many buy-outs do involve high-technology activities.

Types of buy-outs

From recent UK experience it is possible to distil three distinct kinds of buy-outs. These are as follows:

(a) Corporate disposals or 'hive-downs'.
(b) Shareholder repurchases.
(c) Receivership acquisitions.

Corporate disposals or 'hive-downs'

This form of buy-out is by far the most frequent in the United Kingdom. They usually involve the sale of 100% of the business, whether subsidiary, division or operating unit, through its assets alone, the business entity or only the product names, etc. Occasionally, a partial divestment is carried out, with the parent retaining a minority stake in the new entity. This minority holding is often linked to deferred payment terms. The existing management team usually initiates the buy-out, but additional management is sometimes injected at the birth of the independent enterprise.

The major reasons for this form of disposal are similar to those which would encourage the parent company to sell the same activity to another parent. However, there are often feelings of loyalty to the management team, which, if it has sufficient initiative, may be able to achieve first option before the parent proceeds to any sale within the trade. In addition, a strong subsidiary management team seeking independence may not make it easy to sell the subsidiary to another company. There is an element of moral and practical 'blackmail' available to the resident management team if it is sufficiently committed to independence.

Possible reasons for parental divestment include the following:

(a) The parent company is in difficulties.
(b) The subsidiary is peripheral to core business strategy.
(c) The subsidiary is unprofitable but overhead savings are available on buy-out.
(d) Post-merger rationalisation of unwanted parts of an acquisition.
(e) Difficult subsidiary/parent management relationships or parent management overstretch, where limited management resources are required elsewhere in the group, most probably in the mainstream activities.

There are particular advantages in this form of buy-out:

(a) Professional management is already in place.
(b) An established track record is open to investigation.
(c) Management disciplines and controls are established.
(d) There is the opportunity to buy assets at a discount.

There are, however, specific problems that may arise from this form of buy-out after independence:

(a) Management may not be able to withstand the harsh reality of independence.
(b) Vulnerability to markets and suppliers without parent 'protection'.
(c) It may be difficult to make a clean break with the parent, e.g. if the latter is still a supplier, customer, lender or landlord.
(d) Inclination to underestimate past contribution made by the parent.
(e) The parent may not be selling for the reasons stated.

These problems are often manifestations of the fact that membership of a group of companies does provide essential central services, insurance against poor decisions and market credibility, which may not be available to an independent unit. Frequently, the management team and indeed its supporting investors/bankers do not take sufficient account of this fact beforehand.

Shareholder repurchases

An increasingly common buy-out is where the original founder and current owner wishes to retire but does not wish to sell to a trade buyer or seek a stock market listing. In this case the management team, which has often been in effective operational control of the business for a number of years, seeks outside finance to buy out the retiring owner and/or his family interest and thereby become the controlling shareholders themselves. Usually, this would involve gaining control of the ongoing business by purchasing the shares held by the current owner. It may be that the management already has a minority holding and seeks a majority holding through the purchase of this equity with the participation of new investors. In this type of buy-out there is rarely the need for a new banking relationship, the existing bankers remaining in their current position.

Variations on this theme occur when there is a division in family interests or objectives, i.e. part of the ownership of the family company wishes to sell out while the others are prepared to continue in management. Here the investors would seek to repurchase the outgoing family shareholdings. It may also happen that the younger generation of a family business wishes to purchase the previous generation's holding and thereby gain control with the help of new investors. In the case of both these types of continuing family control, it is critical for the new outside investor that the remaining family management is competent to run the business in a professional manner.

The particular advantages of this form of buy-out are as follows:

(a) The same as those for corporate disposals, except asset discount is unlikely.
(b) A creative financial structure can be used to achieve a fiscal advantage for private vendors, while reducing the costs to managers/investors.

Specific problems of this type of buy-out are listed below:

(a) The price may not allow an adequate discount on assets.
(b) A collective vendor often presents difficulties in negotiations.
(c) Management may covet the outgoing vendor's life-style.
(d) The personality of the vendor may be important to the customer and supplier, or in motivation of the management team.

Where a vendor involves more than one member of a family, there are often protracted negotiations over the terms acceptable to each vendor. The management team may simply wish to acquire the 'expensive life-style' enjoyed by the outgoing founder/entrepreneur(s), which is frequently the case in family-owned private companies. The potential investor must also be aware of the possible impact of retirement by the outgoing shareholder on the customer/supplier relationships of the company, which may not be as strong under the remaining management team.

Receivership acquisitions

This is probably the most difficult form of buy-out to achieve. It is a well-tried route by both management and supporting investors but is usually doomed to failure because of the urgency of the receiver's need to realise cash. Another reason is the obvious advantage to a trade buyer in being able to justify a pre-emptive offer due to a detailed knowledge of the business unit for sale – knowledge that is not initially available to the investor.

The reasons why this form of buy-out is pursued are as follows:

(a) The good part of an unattractive group may be available.
(b) Purchase by new management, i.e. 'outsider', is possible.

The main advantages of receivership acquisitions include the following:

(a) There is the opportunity of a 'clean' purchase, excluding liabilities.
(b) New management can be injected from the outset.
(c) Special terms are often achievable.
(d) A choice of assets is available.

There are particular problems in this form of buy-out, however, which make it a greater risk than either of the other two types of buy-out:

(a) Market standing/supplier relations may already be damaged.
(b) The better employees may have gone.
(c) There are higher initial working capital needs.
(d) Trade buyers can often outbid managers/investors.

Key factors for success

To summarise, the key factors in identifying or constructing a potentially successful buy-out are outlined below.

Management commitment/motivation critical. Apart from the need to ensure that the management team is financially committed and stands to lose a serious amount if the buy-out fails, a strong entrepreneurial drive is important to carry the team through any difficult times which lie ahead. Investors often mistake 'professionalism' in a management team for 'entrepreneurism'.

Need for outside experience on board. Non-executive directors of the right calibre will bring immeasurable benefit and essentially replace the advisory/protective role previously exercised by the parent company. The right outside directors can also bring a positive contribution through their industrial contacts, market knowledge or technological background, and are particularly relevant to strategy formulation – in which the team may be relative novices.

Personal relations must be good. The buy-out management must be a tight-knit team of people who are unusually honest with each other while still remaining effective. This is not necessarily the case in a divisional or subsidiary relationship, where parent companies can make management changes at will if strains become apparent.

Balance of team essential, especially in finance. It is important that the team at senior level be in balance, covering each major business function. It may be necessary to hire extra senior management to fill any gaps in the buy-out team.

Cost of deal should allow cash generation from day one. The objective of purchasing assets at a discount is partly to provide future borrowing capacity and also to reduce the initial debt through the sale of surplus assets. In trading terms, however, the buy-out should allow cash generation from the outset rather than requiring major capital expenditure or working capital funding.

Management performance incentive important. Although in many buy-outs it will not be possible for the management to have a majority stake from the outset, an important motivation is the willingness by the investors to allow their holdings to be reduced, possibly even into a minority position. This can be achieved through the issue of extra shares to management or through a lower rate of conversion by the investor syndicate's preferred/preference shares, depending on whether projected targets are reached. An alternative type of incentive is for the management to start at its maximum share stake, with the venture capital investors allowed to convert sufficient preferred shares to dilute the management stake – if management fails to achieve its own forecasts over an agreed period of years.

These arrangements are known as 'ratchets' or 'earn-outs' and are designed to give the management its desired equity holding – if their profit forecasts are achieved – while maintaining the investor's rate of return requirement if forecasts are not achieved. Earn-outs are also used to structure other venture capital investments, particularly in early-stage financings.

In establishing the maximum management stake and consequently the minimum investors' stake, a rule-of-thumb approach has become common, known as the *envy ratio*. This is a simple formula, by which the ratio of investor-to-management financial contribution is divided by the ratio of investor-to-management equity. If the management seeks too disproportionate an equity position in relation to its financial contribution, an investor syndicate may decline to support the buy-out.

Gearing must be minimised, especially early debt repayment/high servicing costs; banker must be a partner. As already mentioned, excess initial debt is often the single major cause of failure in young companies. It is important that when a buy-out is constructed, any clearing-bank lending be on more generous terms concerning security and repayment than is normally the case. To some extent the banker must be prepared to take a quasi-equity risk – not always a comfortable position for the traditional banker. Government grants may also be available to assist with the financing burden.

Tripartite negotiations make buy-outs unusually lengthy/complicated. Unlike other forms of venture capital investment, where normally only two parties are involved, the investor and the investee, the buy-out includes an equally important party, the vendor. The interests of the management team and its investors are usually at one in achieving from the vendor the lowest possible price and the longest possible interest-free deferred payment, but the investors are also keen to arrange a good deal for themselves. The real pressure in a buy-out falls on the management team, which is negotiating a sale with the vendor and often simultaneously a funding package with investors. The management should certainly have its own financial advisers; a number of intermediaries specialising in buy-outs have become established in the United Kingdom, in addition to the major merchant banks and accounting firms that are becoming experienced in this new field of corporate advice.

Trade unions. The parent company's unions often resist a buy-out, as this will weaken their group membership. However, a poor management/union relationship is usually improved after a buy-out because of the closer liaison between operating unit management and shop-floor, in contrast to the tendency of large groups to manage their industrial relations from the centre.

Why can buy-outs fail?

At this stage, with the bulk of UK buy-outs having taken place only since 1980, there is little analytical material on the reasons for failure. It is inevitable, however, that the failure rate will increase as the weaknesses inherent in many buy-outs prove insuperable. The main causes of potential failure include those listed below.

Inadequate (or uncommitted) management team. Frequently a buy-out team goes 'into shock' for the first year or so. Weaknesses in the management team may not become apparent until some time after the buy-out, when external pressures may expose areas which would have been covered by the previous parent company or where back-up management resources could have been made available by the parent.

Inaccurate pre-investment product/market evaluation. Just as with early-stage financings, the investors may well have misjudged or have been misled. The rate of technological change may not have been properly examined either. It is particularly important to ensure that the parent is not divesting because of a long-term declining trend in the health of the buy-out business.

Excessive initial debt gearing. This problem is equally applicable to start-ups, and although there are attractive arguments in favour of investors seeking a secured position in the initial funding, the major cause of failure in any young or high-growth company is the requirement to repay initial debt and particularly to service a high level of debt in the early years of development. Many venture capitalists find a way around this problem by seeking preference stock rather than loans as part of the financial package, with preference stock having a low initial coupon but the right to participate in future profits once a satisfactory level of cash flow and profit generation is achieved. This preference stock would also be long-term, say 10–20 years, with repayment possible over an extended period and usually not during the first five years.

Insufficient cash contingency. It is important that the initial funding includes a substantial contingency against the management's projected cash flow; as much as 50% additional provision may be required.

Disagreement between parties. If a buy-out runs into a difficult period, either through internal inadequacies or external circumstances, the first strains will appear between the management team and its investors. In such a case, it is important that the investor has the commitment and ability to provide 'hands-on' support including, if necessary, the ability to replace members of the management team. Many buy-out investors are not staffed with this in mind and they will undoubtedly have problems with some of their buy-out investments in the years to come.

Equally, it may be that where a syndicate or a consortium of investors is involved, they do not share a common view as to the right solution to any problems that may occur. It is possible that because of this inability to agree a buy-out may fail, although one of the investors is prepared in principle to provide further funds or accept a renegotiation of terms – but will not do so unless the partner investors agree.

Annexe 3 (page 186) gives examples of a number of buy-out structures from ECI's own experience.

Part three The investment process

7 Fund selection: the entrepreneur's choice

The venture capital investment process might be thought to begin with each partner to the potential transaction – entrepreneur and venture capitalist – selecting their preferred investor and investee respectively from the options available. Before the mid-1970s the venture capitalist was generally in control, with a relative lack of competition for those deals he chose to invest in. Counter-selection of venture capital partners by the entrepreneur was rare.

Now the pendulum has swung in the other direction, with a soundly based company or project being able to pick and choose among a host of eager potential investors from the 100 or more active UK venture capital funds. What does, or should, each partner now seek in the other, in the hope and expectation of ensuring a successful and mutually profitable long-term relationship?

A few key aspects of the future relationship between entrepreneur and investor must be investigated by the entrepreneur before a deal is consummated:

(a) The 'hands-on' or 'hands-off' style of the venture capitalist.
(b) The fund's attitude towards deal structuring.
(c) The exit aspirations of the fund.
(d) The fund's financial stability and the availability of follow-up finance.
(e) The fund management's track record, both as individuals and as a team.

Hands-on or hands-off

There are many kinds of entrepreneur, but as far as the venture capitalist is concerned there are two basically opposed categories – those who vehemently resist any perceived involvement by the investor in their business and those who tolerate, and even welcome, a supportive involvement. The *'hands-on'* style of fund will have board representation as an automatic condition of investment. It will also have a close and regular dialogue with the company on matters affecting technology, marketing strategy and senior management assessment. The board representative of the fund, chosen with the entrepreneur's approval, will usually be someone able to make a positive contribution to the business in its technology, products and markets, rather than being primarily a financial 'watch-dog'. In effect, the 'hands-on' fund will form a working partnership with the entrepreneur, which is not normally the case with the *reactive* or *passive* styles of fund.

The entrepreneur resisting involvement is unlikely to seek finance from a fund with a 'hands-on' or actively supportive style and reputation. He may be able to find sources of finance from among the minority of venture capitalists who make a positive virtue of their *'hands-off'* or *passive* post-investment position. These funds will receive only semi-annual or annual information from the company, may have a 'reserve' right to a director and will rarely be in contact with their investees.

There is also an intermediate style of operation, which can best be described as *reactive*. Here the fund will enjoy a flow of information from its investee companies. It will also have certain rights to be consulted on (or even to approve) key decisions, such as major capital expenditure, acquisitions and board appointments. There may or may not be the right to appoint a director to the company's board, but if this right is exercised, the primary role is likely to be that of a financial watch-dog rather than an active contributor to management decisions, which is the case with the 'hands-on' style of fund. The borderline between reactive and 'hands-on' is not always easy to identify.

Where the entrepreneur is either neutral or positive towards involvement by the venture capitalist in his business he should identify which fund management team provides the best match. This will be done through a combination of personal chemistry, the general industrial credentials of the team and their specific technology 'fit' with his own background and aspirations.

Deal-structuring flexibility

Whatever the preferences of the entrepreneur concerning 'hands-on' or 'hands-off', he should seek out the fund that will match most closely his current needs and the long-term requirements of his business as defined by himself and his advisers. Some funds are less willing than others to adapt the conventional deal structures; some are now so flexible in their eagerness to do business that the entrepreneur may not believe the generosity of the terms offered.

The basis of flexibility will be the degree to which the venture capitalist is prepared to provide a package of financial instruments which will neither dominate the entrepreneur's equity nor pre-empt the profits or cash flows of the business. At the core of this equation is the equity valuation of the business, from its past record and future prospects (see Chapter 9).

In testing the intentions of his suitors, the entrepreneur should identify clearly whether the fund's prime objective is a substantial running income yield from the outset or maximum capital gain – or both (some venture capitalists are simply greedy!). Some entrepreneurs may not wish to 'go public' and thus will probably have to prepare himself to compensate the venture capitalist with an attractive income yield plus a premium on redemption of his investment.

Where the entrepreneur is firmly committed to a visible exit – and capital gain for himself – he should be able to achieve a low or nil income cost investment but will have a tough argument over a fair valuation for the business. What will be at issue here is the extent to which the venture capitalist can be persuaded to take account of the entrepreneur's future prospects. A 'fair valuation' in venture capital has a simple meaning – that figure which can be agreed upon between the two parties concerned!

Whatever the deal structure, it will always involve the entrepreneur in allowing an outsider to share in his equity at a significant level. The entrepreneur who objects to this should never approach a venture capitalist for finance. Deal structuring is covered in more specific detail in the Annexes at the end of this book.

Exit aspirations

A common cause of conflict between entrepreneur and venture capitalist is the belated awareness of differences in their exit objectives. The more successful venture capital investments usually have an entrepreneur-driven realisation rather than one decided by the investors, whether through a trade sale, quotation or share repurchase (buy-back).

Most venture capitalists claim to be long-term investors. What the entrepreneur often does not challenge is the particular venture capitalist's definition of long-term! With the resurgence of venture capital since 1980, many are tempted by the apparent opportunities for short-term (1–3 years) capital gains through USM or OTC quotations (see Chapter 11). Although there are likely to be some early USM or OTC realisations, these will be in the minority among venture capital investments, the majority exiting within the industry 'norm' of 3–7 years.

Where the entrepreneur is relaxed about an early exit, then the investor's time horizon is not of great importance. Most entrepreneurs, however, would be well advised to seek out investors whose horizons are basically long-term and to whom an earlier realisation would be a pleasant surprise (if that is what the entrepreneur wants for himself). There have been unhappy experiences in the venture capital industry where entrepreneurs have been persuaded by their investors to seek an early realisation – particularly a share quotation – before the company is sufficiently well founded, with less than satisfactory results for the entrepreneur, his employees and the new investors as the newly quoted company fails to fulfil the market's expectations.

Another aspect of exit conflicts, especially in share quotations (OTC, USM or full listing), is the choice of sponsors for the share issue. The entrepreneur is well advised to seek independent advice, even if his venture capitalists are themselves linked to a particular issuing house, whether merchant bank or stockbroker. The venture capitalist will naturally prefer to introduce the company to the share markets through his own contacts or merchant bank. These sources of advice may be excellent, but the entrepreneur should investigate whether the costs involved are market-related and whether the valuation suggested is the best available, taking a prudent view that the company's share price should hold up after the initial and inevitable speculative interest.

In summary, it is always sensible for entrepreneur and venture capitalist to agree on an exit objective and timescale from the outset of their partnership, and for the entrepreneur to take independent advice when a share quotation is planned.

Fund viability and liquidity

At present there are over 100 separate fund management groups in the UK venture capital industry. Most of these are well founded, supported by major banks or investment institutions, or are BES funds approved by the Department of Trade and Industry and by the Inland Revenue (and hence by the Treasury).

The objectives, stamina and commitment of a venture capital fund's backers are matters not often considered by the entrepreneur when choosing among his potential sources of finance. There will be future problems for venture capital funds that do not themselves have investors with an understanding of the hazards of the business and an appreciation of three basic truths of the venture capital process:

(a) There will be several early failures before big successes are achieved, and the net asset value of the fund may thus decline for the first few years – below the value of the investors' original subscription.
(b) The period before the fund's overall performance can be properly judged will be at least five years, and more usually seven or ten.
(c) It is not enough to invest only once in a promising business. Successful venture capital propositions will frequently require two or more rounds of financing.

An entrepreneur seeking venture capital should identify whether the funds he approaches have committed backers rather than investors looking for an easy sequence of quick realisations at attractive capital gains. The latter will inevitably be disappointed, implying difficulties for the investee company when raising follow-on finance from its original investors prior to realisation.

The availability of *follow-on finance* from the original backers should be of particular importance to an entrepreneur; a number of funds will be 'one-shot' efforts which, when fully invested, may not be able to raise further finance from their backers. Some BES funds may be especially susceptible to this danger, with their emphasis on becoming fully invested on an annual basis and with no certain prospect of further finance being available to a particular fund.

Where the prospective venture capitalist is an offshoot of a larger organisation, it is important that the entrepreneur satisfies himself about the seriousness of the organisation's venture capital effort. How long has it been in the business? What resources, in terms of both people and money, has it committed to venture capital? Has it been in, and out of, the industry before? What are the other motivations of the organisation in establishing a venture capital activity – is it investing primarily for public relations purposes, or to achieve fee income for other parts of its corporate finance business, e.g. new USM or stock market issues, or to provide an outlet for its lending facilities?

Track record of fund and team

As with the questions the venture capitalist will ask of the entrepreneur, so will the entrepreneur want information about his potential backers:

(a) How long have they been in the business, and how successful have they been in backing similar entrepreneurs?
(b) What are the particular objectives of the fund – maximum income or maximum capital growth? Or what emphasis on each reward factor?
(c) How much experience has the fund's management team had in his business sector and technology?
(d) Have the fund's managers any industrial experience, or are they financially experienced people with an orientation towards financial rather than marketing or technological criteria?

Apart from the need to ensure that the chemistry is good between entrepreneur and venture capitalist, the entrepreneur will benefit in good times and particularly in the inevitable bad times from venture capitalist backers with extensive industrial general management experience. It is not necessarily beneficial for an entrepreneur to find backers with specific and detailed expertise in his industry or technology; they may be out of date and can err on the side of excessive second-guessing of the entrepreneur's own judgement.

Finally, the entrepreneur should ensure that there is some stability in his venture capitalist's team. Are they committed full-time to this activity or do they have other responsibilities – which may mean they are not available when he needs advice and guidance. Has the team been together for long or do members move in and out with ominous regularity?

All in all, although the entrepreneur is nowadays in the happy position of being able to pick and choose, the job of fund selection is a difficult one but so important that it must be undertaken seriously.

8 A venture capitalist's selection criteria

A quote one hears frequently when a US venture capitalist is asked how he selects investment propositions is 'Management first, management second and management again.'

Selection of early-stage investments

Management, or the entrepreneur plus his team (if he has one), is really all the venture capitalist has to go on when looking at early-stage financings. The products may not yet exist, with the potential markets undeveloped and the technology not yet established. It will be difficult to discover in any meaningful detail what competitors exist, even through extensive patent searching.

What the entrepreneur must prove, in these circumstances, is that he has a credible business plan, ensuring that his own (and his team's) track record gives the venture capitalist confidence that he can achieve the plan. Nothing is certain at this stage in the business's history – whether seed, start-up or second-round – and the venture capitalist will be screening many propositions to choose those that provide the required risk/reward ratio. Because of the inherent uncertainty, this ratio is not an arithmetic equation but rather a balance of judgement. Has the business a better than 50% chance of success with that particular management team? If it succeeds, can there be a minimum five times multiple of the investors' original investment? This will be the prime objective of the venture capitalist, since most of his investments will fall short of a satisfactory return and as many as half may fail altogether. Each prospective investment must be measured against this return-on-investment target, which usually equates to an internal rate of return of 25% minimum. Only those projects which can convince the investors of their likelihood of achieving this target will normally receive finance, at least from commercially focused venture capital sources.

Business plan evaluation

The professionalism (or lack of it) of his business plan is the first thing by which an entrepreneur will be judged. Often the venture capitalist will not yet have met the entrepreneur, although it is advisable that an early meeting takes place, with the business plan presented in person by the entrepreneur, so that each party can form an initial (and often enduring) impression of the other. Such a first meeting may well establish a mutual respect between the two parties, which can overcome inadequacies in the entrepreneur's business plan if the venture capitalist is sufficiently impressed by the entrepreneur. The ability of the entrepreneur to engineer this 'dry run' will depend on his own persuasiveness, that of his financial advisers (see Chapter 9), and also on how comparatively attractive are the other proposals the venture capitalist is currently examining.

The entrepreneur's plan will provide the focus for the venture capitalist's own detailed investigations into the business. This means that the more comprehensive the plan, the shorter the decision time for the investor – provided, of course, that there are no fundamental discrepancies between the entrepreneur's claims and the venture capitalist's own findings.

There is no exact formula for a business plan,* but any such plan should include these key points:

(a) A brief history of the business or project.
(b) A synopsis of the career histories of the entrepreneur and his key managers.
(c) A description of the business's products or services, their markets (including growth prospects) and the present or likely competition.
(d) A summary of the technology involved, including manufacturing processes, and a review of the likely threats from technological obsolescence or competing new technologies.
(e) A financial history (if any) and forward projections of turnover, profits, cash flow and borrowings over at least a two-year period.
(f) If possible, the entrepreneur's (or his advisers') proposed deal structure for the funding sought, together with any preliminary views on his preferred exits.

* A practical and thorough explanation of the business plan format is available in a booklet produced by Arthur Andersen & Co. in conjunction with the British Venture Capital Association.

It is frequently useful to have an 'Executive Summary' as well as a full business plan, in which the highlights of the proposal can be covered briefly. Similarly, rather than a somewhat intimidating business plan of 100 pages or more, it is common for detailed tables, forecasts, product or patent data and market research statistics to be presented as a separate 'volume of appendices'.

The key areas for investigation will include the following:

(a) The track record of the entrepreneur and his management team (see below).
(b) The technical performance assumptions about the product/process/service.
(c) The market size, growth and penetration (market share and distribution effectiveness) assumptions.
(d) The price/cost assumptions, particularly with regard to competition.
(e) The staff resources assumption, with special attention to the mix, source and cost of essential skills.
(f) The overall timescale and important milestones along the business's anticipated path.

Clearly, the project's financial projections will also be evaluated in detail by the venture capitalist, possibly with investigating accountants, and the proposed financial control system will be closely appraised.

Each investment proposal will have special features which will be regarded as critical, but some elements of technology or marketing are likely to be common in their importance:

(a) How compressed are product life cycles in the business sector concerned? Does the particular project contain its seeds for the next generation or is it a one-shot effort?
(b) How much does success depend on the product/process/service being first into the market? If it must be first, will it be?
(c) Is the market likely to be ready for the product/process/service, or is the project ahead of its time?
(d) How much is known of international competition, either present or potential?
(e) Can the business be easily adapted to provide for exploitation in peripheral markets of greater long-term potential?
(f) Does the business have all the technological ingredients for success, or is there a missing link in the chain from the original research to

the market-place. Is the entrepreneur willing to buy in this knowledge, which may be readily available elsewhere?

(g) If a realistic provision is made for the doubling up of both time and cost, does the project still meet the required targets?

(h) Is the project viable only on a full assembly or production and market basis or can it be licensed out or franchised, with lower risks but adequate rewards? Is the entrepreneur prepared to contemplate this possibility or is he determined to go it alone?

As far as the general areas of investigation mentioned are concerned, there are checklists galore available from management consultants, accountancy firms, business schools and textbooks, covering all aspects of business. It will serve no purpose simply to reproduce these here; the experienced venture capitalist will have his own checklist, validated through practical experience.

Whether the entrepreneur's short list of venture capitalists includes high-technology funds or not, the potential investor(s) may have to seek specialist technical or marketing appraisal from outside experts. Clearly, this may cause the entrepreneur concern, for reasons of confidentiality, although if proper secrecy agreements are in force there should be no real risk from competitors. Frequently, the outside expert will be at a university or research institute, and the project may thus actually benefit from the specialist appraisal.

The venture capitalist will himself wish to check potential customers and key suppliers, in addition to making the usual inquiries of current bankers and auditors, and previous employers of the management team.

Management assessment

In judging the quality of the entrepreneur and his team, the primary question for a venture capitalist is whether the entrepreneur is an able technologist or solely an opportunist businessman – or both. A combination of these two qualities is often a recipe for success, but if the entrepreneur is solely an inventor, with little or no business management experience, the business is usually ill-fated. If business opportunism dominates, then there is frequently insufficient substance to the project to make it a real success.

A 'hands-on' or active venture capitalist can 'marry' an able technologist or inventor to a recruited, proven business manager – provided, of course, the entrepreneur will accept such a partnership.

The UK venture capital industry is likely to be littered increasingly with failed investments, where the entrepreneur was not a businessman but believed he was. Only a 'hands-on' venture capitalist is likely to be able to step in and save such a project from disaster. Unfortunately for the United Kingdom in this respect, there are proportionately fewer combined inventor/businessman entrepreneurs than in the United States. The causes are largely historical, arising from the United Kingdom's consistent educational and social bias against industry and business in favour of the professions, science and the civil service. Only now are there signs of a change in this anti-entrepreneurial ethos, with many of today's new entrepreneurs – not surprisingly – having had their earlier careers in the UK subsidiaries of North American corporations.

The management performance records of the entrepreneur's team will be critically examined by the venture capitalist, both as to their specific suitability for the particular business and as to their past achievements. The venture capitalist will be looking for two additional factors, peculiar to this new industry: first, the individual commitment of each team member to the business, as evidenced by his financial risk and the career (and job security) sacrifices he has made; and second, the personality 'fit' of the team members, which is critical in that they must be able to complement each other, back up one another function-ally, and pull together in times of difficulty rather than pull apart.

It is even the practice in certain venture capital partnerships to put the entrepreneur and his team through a several-day 'mental assault course' to assess their compatibility as well as their suitability as entrepreneurial managers. This approach is not an essential part of the selection process with all funds.

Apart from technical skills, the venture capitalist is looking for marketing expertise, financial planning and control disciplines, and above all energy, drive and motivational ability in the team leader.

Later-stage investments

Much of the description of the process of early-stage selection will apply equally to the venture capitalist's evaluation of the more mature business seeking finance for expansion, buy-out, 'money out' or turn-around. In particular, the evaluation of the business's market position and potential, its technology and the professionalism of its business plan still apply.

A double advantage applies to judgement of the later-stage venture compared with early-stage proposals. First, there is an established business trajectory by which to judge the quality of financial performance, technology (if any) and product/market position. In addition, the markets in which the business operates are generally more stable and predictable. Market data are often plentiful and the relative competitive positions in the industry are usually well known. There is adequate and detailed information on the various aspects of the business's past performance, including its ability to achieve budgets and its financial control procedures.

Second, the management's track record is clearly identifiable, both for the team and for individuals. The 'team fit' can be more easily assessed than in early-stage projects, and it is usually easier to replace individual team members as they move on or prove to be inadequate in their performance. The management team is likely to have a formal structure and, although there will be a leader, he is unlikely to be as dominant a personality as in the newer early-stage business.

The rate of failure in later-stage venture capital investments is low, and this form of equity financing is significantly safer than early-stage finance if proposals are properly investigated and prudently structured from the outset. Equally, however, there are fewer 'big winners' among the more mature businesses. The venture capitalist in this area of activity is likely to seek a solid income yield on his investment from the outset and may also provide secured lending as part of the financing package. A good cash flow and secure assets are characteristics of these investments, and in most cases the investor will be prepared to provide only one round of financing before realisation. By comparison, in the typical early-stage proposal a venture capitalist expects to – and the entrepreneur will expect him to – provide successive rounds of finance until the project or business succeeds or fails.

Sensitivity analysis and downside assessment

A professional venture capitalist will not invest unless he has carried out a 'downside' or prudent assessment of the business's future prospects, usually by himself but sometimes with outside help from investigating accountants and/or consultants. The objective is to be satisfied that, on the 'worst case' set of assumptions, the project or business would still be viable and give an adequate investment return.

Venture capital experience dictates that no budget or forecast is ever exactly on target; sometimes it is exceeded, but rarely. More commonly, the business underperforms on sales and margins but overruns cost and overhead assumptions. The net result of either over- or underachievement of budget is usually an increasing cash requirement.

In the early-stage business, sales success means cash shortage due to higher-than-predicted working capital requirements, as well as fixed-asset expenditure ahead of plan. Failure to meet budget often means cash deficits to pay for losses persisting longer than anticipated.

The more mature, later-stage business may actually create cash surpluses if it grows faster than expected, because of adequate margins, a stable market position, reduced competitive threats and a cost base under control. Further, its growth rate, if successful, is unlikely to be of the same magnitude as a successful newer business; hence lower incremental working capital requirements.

If a later-stage business underperforms, it usually has a certain amount of 'fat' to shed before further cash is required. If it has a heavy gearing in its debt/equity structure, however – as is the case in many management buy-outs – it may require a substantial equity transfusion to survive and gain a second chance to prosper.

A sensitivity analysis is a rigorous testing of the implications of sales or market shortfalls and cost or capital overruns – a key part of the venture capitalist's assessment procedure. In carrying out a sensitivity analysis of the entrepreneur's business plan, the venture capitalist will give particular consideration to the following aspects:

(a) Realism of sales forecasts by product and market sector.
(b) Key new product launches and disproportionate profit contributions by minority activities and product lines.
(c) Gross margin or value added assumptions.
(d) Working capital usage; stock, debtor and creditor turnover.
(e) Interest rate assumptions.
(f) Adequacy of physical capacity and the cost of additions.
(g) Labour flexibility, availability and the state of industrial relations.
(h) Likely competitive reaction to the entrepreneur's strategy.

The kind of 'what if' questions the venture capitalist asks of himself can be typified by the following:

(a) What would be the effect of a sales shortfall of 5%, 10%, 15% or 20%?
(b) What would be the result of value added or gross contribution at 40%, 45% or 50% rather than 60%?
(c) What would be the impact on cash flow if net working capital (stock plus debtors minus creditors) runs at 25% or 30% of sales rather than 20%?

(d) What would be the profitability and cash flow effects of major contracts falling later, or earlier, than expected?

(e) How serious would be the possibility of inadequate availability of staff with the right skills mix, and what would be the impact?

At the end of the day, the venture capitalist will probably not tell the entrepreneur the outcome of his downside assessment, but it is almost certain that he will be comparing actual results with his assessment – alongside, or even in place of, the entrepreneur's own forecasts or budgets.

The downside assessment may spur the venture capitalist to insist on a larger cash and equity injection, or less debt in the deal structure, than is required in the view of the entrepreneur and his advisers. In such cases, the venture capitalist may decline to invest because the business would be undercapitalised from the outset – even if it has clear attractions in its growth potential. This is one of the traditional problems of UK venture capital: the resistance by the entrepreneur to equity dilution beyond his own chosen limit, even if a greater dilution were to give the business a better chance to achieve his sought-for success.

This is the kind of situation where the venture capitalist will use the simple but telling argument that, say, 55% of a £1 million business should be more attractive to the entrepreneur than 70% of a £½ million business or 90% of a failed business. Such rational argument does not, regrettably, always win against the UK entrepreneur's traditional determination to preserve, as far as possible, his absolute control over the business which he founded.

In the United States, by contrast, there is a much greater willingness to forgo equity percentage in return for a larger eventual valuation and cash realisation. Fortunately, there are signs that the currently emerging generation of UK entrepreneurs is beginning to recognise the benefits of accepting the venture capitalist's simple argument.

9 Negotiating the deal

Negotiations start from the entrepreneur's first approach to his chosen venture capitalist(s). Thereafter, each meeting, telephone discussion, telex and letter is itself a mini-negotiation in a unique process which is part courtship, part mutual trial by equals and part poker game.

Timescale

How long does the selection and negotiation process take? It depends on a variety of factors: the quality of the original business plan; the plausibility of the entrepreneur and his team; the age of the technology or the business; and the intensity of international competition. A key factor is the experience and professionalism of the entrepreneur's financial advisers, if any.

Another important influencing factor is the size of investment. Venture capitalists are, after all, also human, and a £100,000 risk investment is not going to absorb the same degree of 'due diligence' or investigation as one of £1 million.

In practice, the time spectrum from arrival of business plan to financial commitment by the venture capitalist can range from one month to one year. Instant decisions in this hazardous business are usually wrong decisions. After the entrepreneur and venture capitalist have come to an agreement, additional time is required by the lawyers on either side. Daunting to both entrepreneur and venture capitalist, legal discussions can add a month or more to the basic agreement already reached between the two principals.

Advisers: their role

It is unusual for an entrepreneur to conduct all the negotiations by himself. He may make the initial approach to a number of potential backers, but there will come a time, earlier rather than later in the process, when the benefits of an independent, experienced adviser will become apparent. These benefits relate to a number of key areas; they can speed up the process and lead to a good match between entrepreneur and venture capitalist. The key areas include:

(a) 'coaching' the business, especially with regard to adequate financial controls;
(b) preparation of a professional business plan;
(c) the selection of a short list of 'best fit' venture capitalists for serious discussions;
(d) valuing the business, designing the preferred deal structure and advising on the financial and tax implications of the venture capitalist's counter-proposals;
(e) handling routine but detailed inquiries from the venture capitalist, and standing in for the entrepreneur at the interminable drafting meetings held towards the end of the process to agree on details and iron out last-minute 'humps'.

Coaching

Even in a completely new business, or seed capital project, there are 'good housekeeping' aspects of the structure and business plan which will help to convince a venture capitalist of the entrepreneur's organisational ability. In essence, these include well-thought-out financial controls and credible supporting data for product costs and fixed-asset expenditure (for plant and buildings). A young business may not yet have developed these disciplines, and the part a financial or accounting adviser can play in shaping up these aspects of a business can make an important contribution to the entrepreneur's overall credibility with his potential backers.

In seeking 'coaching' advice, usually from an accountancy firm, the entrepreneur can expect, at modest cost, sound guidance on matters such as the need to recruit a full-time qualified financial controller or finance director.

'Coaching' advice applies particularly to the early-stage business, which has not yet raised permanent capital beyond the entrepreneur's own resources and those of his bankers. At the later stages, a business will often have adequate organisational structure and financial controls. It will always pay, however, for the management of a mature business to seek its auditors' objective advice on the state of internal disciplines prior to approaching potential venture capital backers for expansion, buy-out or turnaround finance.

Business plan

There is no substitute for a professional business plan, prepared by the entrepreneur and his team. It always raises doubts about an entrepreneur's ability to follow through an effective business strategy if he cannot also plan out that strategy, provide tangible arguments for its likelihood of success, and accurately identify the resources of people, money and time required to implement his plans.

It is standard practice for a professional venture capitalist to find out how much of a business plan presented to him is the entrepreneur's own work and how much that of his adviser. If largely the adviser's, the venture capitalist's questioning of the entrepreneur will be that much more rigorous, to test his originality, aptitude and commitment. That being said, it is frequently true that an adviser makes a useful contribution to the entrepreneur's plan. The part an adviser can play is a combination of testing the entrepreneur's key assumptions, validating the basic figures and generally polishing the plan's presentation.

Investor short list

The right financial adviser will have had extensive experience of the venture capital community. He will know the project preferences of most funds and also – most importantly – their flexibility, professionalism and response time. It can save the entrepreneur much abortive door-knocking and many preliminary discussions if he consults an experienced financial adviser early on. This is particularly the case with the larger project, when a group of investors is required to form a syndicate. The adviser can also 'test the water' for the entrepreneur with a number of potential backers so that he can concentrate his time and effort on serious discussions with a limited number of the most interested venture capitalists. In addition, the adviser can be an objective judge of the best fit between entrepreneur and investor, particularly with regard to such key aspects as 'hands-on' or 'hands-off' style.

Much as investors would prefer it otherwise, it will pay the entrepreneur to have parallel negotiations with more than one potential backer – at least until he has a firm commitment on acceptable terms.

Valuation and designing the structure

A business is almost always worth more in the owner's eyes than in those of potential purchasers. This is also true of venture capital, where the entrepreneur will have expectations of profits performance that a more prudent investor might not share, taking a realistic downside view. Even if the venture capitalist is persuaded of the profit potential, he is unlikely to accept the entrepreneur's view of the appropriate profits multiple to be applied in arriving at a valuation for the business.

Frequently the entrepreneur will look at the current valuations of USM or fully listed businesses with established performance records, and will quite genuinely seek to apply their profits multiples to his own business. Such an approach is unlikely to find favour with a commercial venture capitalist, who is basing his own valuation on the requirement to earn an internal rate of return (IRR) of 25% minimum up until realisation. The realisation value he takes results from a realistic profits multiple applied to his downside projection of profits at realisation, usually assuming a USM or full listing rather than a trade sale. The role of the adviser is to help the entrepreneur adjust psychologically to a reasonable valuation, which will be below his initial expectations, while achieving the best deal possible in the venture capital market at the time.

The adviser will be aware that the venture capitalist includes two components in his IRR calculations – probable capital gain and running income yield. He may be able to design a deal structure alongside that of the venture capitalist which provides the latter with a high income yield to balance any perceived overvaluation of the equity. It is not possible to bridge a wide valuation gap in this way, since most venture capitalists look primarily to the capital gain component in their IRR.

The multiples mentioned above are usually price/earnings (P/E) ratios, which are arrived at by dividing the valuation of the issued ordinary shares (the business's equity) by the post-tax profits after preference dividends – if any. There is a debate at present as to whether the post-tax profits should be calculated after a notional full tax charge or after actual taxes, but that does not affect the basic principle involved. A more long-standing point at issue is which year's profits are to be valued. The entrepreneur, naturally, seeks to push the valuation date as far into the future as possible so that prospective profits of some years' distance are used as the basis for any equity valuation. In practice, as long as the apparent potential returns to the venture capitalist meet his IRR criteria, he may accept a valuation of prospective earnings up to 12 months ahead – particularly if the business is currently unprofitable or just at break-even point, as are many early-stage investments.

In venture capital investment, asset-based valuations are meaningless in early-stage financings, although they may be used as a secondary basis for valuation in later-stage financings, particularly buy-outs.

It is rare for the entrepreneur to be experienced at deal structuring, in the corporate finance sense, or to know the rules of the venture capital game. Here, the financial adviser can propose a deal structure to the entrepreneur that provides him with the optimum: basically, the maximum equity funding possible within the business plan's needs, together with the minimum equity dilution for the entrepreneur.

An 'ideal' deal structure having been agreed with the entrepreneur, it is important for the adviser to be present at all meetings where the structure is discussed with potential backers in order to interpret for the entrepreneur the implications of any variations they propose. It is most unusual, in this context, for there *not* to be some changes in the original structure proposed before negotiations are completed.

The entrepreneur is likely to find, on his short list of backers, a spectrum of deal structure preferences – which means it is important for him to be certain he is comparing like with like before making a final decision. Here the adviser's role is that of corporate finance interpreter or translator.

Investor liaison

There will, of course, be an inevitable flow of requests for detailed information by the venture capitalist(s), and it can help the entrepreneur if the adviser acts as intermediary here – the entrepreneur still having a business to run and his livelihood to earn. A dialogue between prospective investor and adviser will also give an experienced venture capital adviser the opportunity to assess the various backers' continuing interest in the entrepreneur's proposal.

In his liaison capacity, the adviser comes into his own when syndication by a number of venture capitalists is necessary. Both in the original selection of the syndication group, and in handling their various requirements, the right adviser will be invaluable to the entrepreneur.

However, an entrepreneur should control all major aspects of the negotiation process – from his side of the table at least. This means he should be present at important meetings with his backer(s), and handle directly the key parts of their investigations.

Choosing the adviser

When the entrepreneur decides to run his proposal without a financial adviser, as is the case in rare circumstances (where, for example, he is experienced in corporate finance or has dealt successfully with venture capitalists before), he will still need tax and legal advice before completion unless he is prepared to take inadvisable risks. Here he may be able to find both types of advice from a commercial lawyer, rather than hire both a legal adviser and an accounting firm. It will not be particularly important that the entrepreneur gets on well with his advisers, since there is only a limited advisory role to play. The entrepreneur's own auditor is always involved to some extent as well, even if he cannot provide the necessary specialist tax advice.

Another occasion when the entrepreneur may dispense with an adviser until the completion stage of a deal is where the deal has arisen from an approach to the entrepreneur by a venture capitalist. The entrepreneur may be persuaded of the benefits of a deal proposed by such a venture capitalist without seeking alternative offers or taking independent advice. In this case, he will be likely to resort to legal and tax advice only. Still unusual in the United Kingdom, this strategy is being followed by a limited number of funds, frequently specialising in high-technology investments. As the market becomes more competitive, more funds may adopt this approach.

In the majority of venture capital proposals, the entrepreneur will choose his adviser *before* setting out to raise finance. If he has an existing business, his first call is likely to be on his present auditors. He may also ask his local bank manager for recommendations as to where to go for advice. The branch manager is most unlikely to be prepared to give formal advice himself because of the clear conflict of interest. He should, however, know which of the local accountancy or legal firms are the most appropriate to the entrepreneur's particular needs. A bank will usually introduce the entrepreneur to two or three alternative firms of professional advisers, leaving the final choice to the entrepreneur. If the proposed financing is large enough, the branch manager may introduce the entrepreneur to his bank's corporate advice or merchant banking arm.

Sometimes the entrepreneur will wish to avoid informing his bank, at too early a stage, that he is seeking venture capital – in which case his business contacts should be able to help him to locate the major local firms of accountants and commercial solicitors. He should also consider local stockbrokers who can demonstrate venture capital experience, and any regional office of the City merchant banks, although the latter are rarely the least expensive sources of advice.

For the larger deals, particularly syndications and management buy-outs, it may be important to include a stockbroker or merchant banker in the advisory team, as well as an accountant or lawyer. This is usually necessary only when the amount is in excess of £2 million or £3 million, in which case the overall cost of advice clearly will be more expensive.

Whatever the source of advice, the entrepreneur should approach his selection of an adviser as he would the supply of products, raw materials or other business services. In particular, he should find out whether the adviser has in-depth experience of the venture capital industry, how previous entrepreneur-clients regard him, and what sort of reputation he has in the local business community. It is also important that the personal chemistry of entrepreneur and adviser be good, given that they will be spending substantial amounts of time together on a highly significant decision for the entrepreneur's future.

In most cases, the technical complexities of venture capital advice fall on the side of finance and tax rather than law until the completion stages, when the lawyers come to the fore. Typically, therefore, an entrepreneur will choose an adviser from the accounting profession. On the other hand, some members of the legal profession are equally competent on the financial and commercial aspects.

Syndication

In many instances the amount of funding required in a venture capital investment is of such magnitude that a single investor would have majority control of the business – if debt gearing is not to become excessive. This is rarely acceptable to the entrepreneur and to most venture capitalists. It is usual in such a transaction for there to be more than one investor, each with a minority shareholding.

A further reason for syndications is the concept innate in most venture capitalists' strategies of risk diversification through a wide spread of investments. No investor wishes to be over-exposed in any one investment, whether in terms of shareholding or amount at risk. There is also mutual benefit in a syndicated investment, arising from the combined experiences of the partners. This is relevant both to evaluation of the business pre-investment and to post-investment after-care, where it is in all investors' interests to ensure maximum success of the investment's performance.

For venture capital investments with a transaction value in excess of £1 million, it is unusual for a single fund to provide the entire amount. This single-investor cut-off level can be as low as £300,000, particularly when the risks are unusually high. The same holds true for first-round financings, such as seed and start-up projects, where the investors will most likely have to follow on with second-round finance.

Syndicates can include as many as 5–10 venture capital funds in large buy-outs and later-stage expansion financings of £5 million and more. It is possible to invest effectively through such large syndications only if there is a leader of the investment group. The leader can be the principal investor or the financial adviser to the project, such as a merchant bank – provided the adviser is also an investor (to be credible to the other investors). In smaller syndicates of 2–4 investors, it is not yet common practice in the United Kingdom for there to be a clearly identifiable leader. This is contrary to established practice in the United States, where there is almost invariably a syndicate leader (who may be a follower in someone else's syndicate on another occasion).

The main advantages of having a syndicate leader rather than a group of separate investors are as follows:

(a) The leader carries the responsibility for most of the liaison with the entrepreneur and his advisers; this avoids the necessity of dealing at length with each investor, to the detriment of the business and of the entrepreneur's patience.

(b) The leader will negotiate the broad structure of the deal at an early stage, acting as a buffer between the entrepreneur and the other investors; their views will be sought but they will not each be permitted to re-invent the package, as frequently occurs when there is no clear leader.

(c) The leader will carry the brunt of the investigation workload, including the briefing of external accountants and consultants after consultation with the other investors. Each investor will not thus carry out a separate investigation, which would be excessively costly in terms of everyone's time and effort.

(d) Once the investment is made, the leader will continue to spearhead the aftercare activity; usually only he will have board representation and the 'hands-on' role. This will obviate the need for a continuing dialogue with each member of the investing group.

There is not yet enough mutual respect and trust in the UK venture capital industry to make for a smooth operation of syndication. In the main this is an indication of the relative youth of the industry, but it also reflects the innate competitive (rather than collaborative) ethos that persists in UK venture capital.

The climate for syndication will no doubt improve over the medium term, but in the meantime the entrepreneur and his advisers should be firm when handling syndicated investments – insisting, if there is no apparent leader, that they deal largely with one spokesperson of the investing group rather than with each investor in turn. Even with a syndicate leader, most investors will at the very least want to meet and assess the entrepreneur and his team, and to interrogate the leader on his investigation brief and its findings. Syndication is a well-trodden path in the City of London as far as listed company money-raising operations are concerned. There is every expectation that the UK venture capital industry can emulate the flexibility of the 'senior market' in this respect.

Completion

Unless he is an accountant or lawyer (unlikely), the entrepreneur must prepare himself for an entirely frustrating and, to him, fruitless period before the deal is completed, but after agreement in principle has been reached with the venture capital fund.

The venture capitalist will have been through the usually protracted completion process before, and may well have developed standard legal forms of subscription or shareholders' agreement and warranties which can be adapted easily to most investment transactions. Even where this is the case, however, there will remain a need for such items as specific warranties and indemnities, disclosure letters and amended articles of association to accommodate the new classes of financing instrument to be issued, as well as any other special requirements of the venture capitalist.

The time delay between heads of agreement (or agreement in principle) and completion is measured in weeks, rather than months – but it is rarely ever days. This is the period when the lawyers have their say, assisted by the auditors or reporting accountants when necessary.

The entrepreneur must not entirely surrender the fine tuning of the subscription agreement's drafting process to his legal and financial advisers. He should insist on a clear explanation of the exact meaning and implications of the legalities, as he may otherwise not fully understand what concessions or compromises he is making, or being asked to make, by his prospective investors.

The *disclosure letter* is a critical piece of the completion jigsaw. It is a standard practice, in response to the potential investors' need of specific warranties and indemnities, to identify whether there is anything material to the venture capitalist's investment decision that has not yet been mentioned by the entrepreneur and his advisers. In particular, this procedure should flush out any current or pending litigation, unsatisfactory patent protection, inadequate pension provision or insurance cover and other hitherto undisclosed liabilities – as well as any trading matters relating to dependence on key customers or limited sources of raw materials and vital components.

General *warranties* will be sought, similar to those common in purchase and sale agreements, to confirm that:

(a) the audited accounts are correct and still hold true in all material respects at completion;

(b) the capital structure of the business is as shown in the accounts, and no other rights to share capital exist that would dilute the incoming investors' shareholding position;

(c) any information provided to the investors is believed to be accurate, and no material information has been withheld;

(d) any forecasts have been properly prepared, on reasonable assumptions which have not since been overtaken by events;

(e) all special arrangements between the company and its shareholders (and their families) have been disclosed.

Indemnities relating to tax liabilities at the last audit date are also usually sought as a matter of standard practice. Sometimes indemnities concerning any tax liabilities which have arisen from transactions outside the normal course of business since the audit are also sought, e.g. tax-shelter leasing and commodity or currency speculation.

The venture capitalist will seek protective rights as a minority investor through a *subscription or shareholders' agreement* and changes to the company's *articles of association*. Most features of such minority rights can be covered within the articles, but some venture capital funds still expect a weighty subscription agreement as well. This expectation may be somewhat misguided, as a subscription agreement does not carry the legal force of the articles. Breach of the provisions of a subscription agreement are normally subject only to damages, while the articles can be so written as to be unalterable except with the support of the minority shareholders, namely the venture capitalists. The usual method is to define whatever minority protection is agreed within the class rights of the venture capitalists' specific financial instruments, whether these are ordinary or preference shares, or loan stock. The class rights of each instrument are usually then enshrined in the articles of association.

The rights to be built into the articles and/or subscription agreement include those:

(a) ensuring the implementation of the proposed new capital structure, to cover both the immediate effects and any deferred equity rights, through convertible instruments or options;

(b) covering pre-emption rights, applying both to existing and in-coming shareholders;

(c) providing constraints upon sale of a controlling shareholding unless all shareholders benefit equally from the sale;

(d) securing the appointment of a director(s) representing the interests of the investors, and ensuring a flow of management information to the investors;

(e) specifying a series of items on which the venture capital investors' views must be sought and/or their approval given, including major capital expenditure items, top management appointments, changes in the nature of the business, alterations to borrowing powers, share capital, and dividend policy.

Of necessity, this can be only a summary of the ingredients of the final stages of negotiation prior to completion. There is much patience and constructive tolerance required at this last stage – which is also the first stage in what is hoped will be a mutually profitable association. The quality and experience of both sides' legal and financial advisers is of fundamental importance to a successful conclusion.

10 Life after investment

Venture capital investments are illiquid. This means two things: first, the investor cannot simply sell out of his investment if its performance disappoints – or, worse, if it looks like it might fail; second, he will not receive any worthwhile return from his investment for a number of years.

Both these fundamental constraints on a venture capitalist make him concentrate his attention and effort on the performance of his investment to a greater extent than if it were on the listed share market. Apart from the unusual mix of skills and limitless time required, investment aftercare in the venture capital industry requires a continuing close partnership with the entrepreneur. This relationship is of a nature not seen in any other branch of the financial services industry, whether it be lending, merchant banking, leasing, insurance, stockbroking or funds management of listed securities.

Chapter 7 briefly described the contrast between the 'hands-on' and other styles of post-investment aftercare. How does the 'hands-on' approach work in practice?

Hands-on aftercare

The reason for practising this approach to venture capital investment is not simply nosiness or an instinctive desire to interfere with management. It is, basically, the enhancement of the investment, by 'adding value' to the business during the course of its development to improve its rate of volume growth and its profitability. Protection of the downside is also important in the event that the business fails, by a significant margin, to meet the investors' expectations.

The 'hands-on' venture capitalist is somewhat akin to a permanent strategy and technology consultant, with a serious financial commitment to the business. Because of the venture capitalist's self-interest, this is a low-cost consulting facility, with modest fees charged and no likelihood (as is common with traditional consultancy) of abandoning the entrepreneur if he either does not agree with the venture capitalist's views or is uncertain about implementation.

The most important areas of contribution by an effective hands-on venture capitalist will be:

(a) *marketing strategy*, including an informed view of international threats and opportunities in the sectors where the business operates;
(b) *technology development*, depending on the specific technical competence of the venture capitalist's representative in any particular investment;
(c) *long-term business planning* in terms of the eventual goal of the enterprise, including acquisitions and exit policy;
(d) *management structuring* and key staff recruitment and motivation;
(e) *financial planning*, to guide the company through the peaks and troughs of its funding needs.

To execute his task successfully, the hands-on venture capitalist must have an unusual personal competence in addition to his professional and technical skills; he must be a diplomat. To participate effectively in these sensitive areas is to 'shadow' the entrepreneur in all his key tasks. Persuasion and personal chemistry are the required tools, rather than the weapons of insistence and interference. Typical situations where a hands-on venture capitalist becomes actively involved are described more fully below.

Marketing

When a new product launch is planned, or competitors jump the market with a rival product, the venture capitalist is often able, through his knowledge of the product/market area and his international contacts, to bring a valuable perspective to the entrepreneur's decisions in this area. Equally, it can be the case that the venture capitalist picks up advance intelligence about specific market threats and opportunities, especially in the fast-changing world of high technology. This is usually possible because the high-tech venture capital fund has tentacles in many peripheral areas of the relevant technologies – while the entrepreneur and his team tend to specialise within a comparatively narrowly defined sector, where they clearly will be more expert than the venture capitalist.

A further area of marketing where the hands-on venture capitalist can help is cross-fertilisation between different businesses in his portfolio. At its simplest, this may be through the introduction of portfolio members to each other as potential customers or suppliers for each other's products or services. A more complex form of such cross-fertilisation can be where one investment's technology can be transferred to another through licensing for a royalty or through joint ventures. This is not possible when the businesses are direct competitors (this is an unlikely and infrequent occurrence anyway) but can be relevant where one company's technology has important peripheral applications.

Such marketing add-ons are clearly more likely when the venture capital fund itself has international links, particularly in the United States and Japan – both major sources of today's and tomorrow's competitive technology. It must not be forgotten that UK technology markets account for only 5% of those available worldwide.

Technology

Apart from the 'window on technology' that the hands-on venture capital fund can provide, its board representative often has direct and recent experience of the technology or industry sector in which the business operates. The entrepreneur thus has a second and possibly expert opinion to draw on from his own board.

Where the venture capital fund has close relations with universities or research institutes, the board representative may come from an academic institution and may be able to make a particularly valuable contribution. Often such a fund's academic or research relationships can be used to good effect in providing key 'missing linkages' in the entrepreneur's applications technology – without which the business or project may not succeed.

In certain cases, the technical expertise of the venture capitalist is such that he is able to rescue a failing investment, where the entrepreneur himself is unable to turn it round. This will, of course, require general management and financial expertise as well as technical skills.

Business policy

The venture capitalist with a hands-on style will almost always have had general management experience, possibly including a period in industrial consulting. The entrepreneur may often have had no general management experience at all, and may never have acquired another business. He is also most unlikely to have had dealings with the stock market and thus will lack a familiarity with company valuation and with his own exit options.

Here the involved venture capitalist is in his element in that he has a genuinely independent role to play rather than shadowing or 'second-guessing' the entrepreneur – which may appear to be the case with his marketing or technology inputs. The entrepreneur will come to rely upon an experienced venture capitalist in matters of acquisition valuation, negotiation and exit strategy (see Chapter 11).

The hands-on venture capital fund will also have connections in the financial advisory community which the entrepreneur will normally lack. The venture capitalist can thus designate the most appropriate from among the many advisory firms that will vie for the entrepreneur's 'account'.

Management

In many venture capital projects the entrepreneur will start with a small team of committed colleagues and may not have much experience of recruitment and assessment of key staff. An experienced venture capitalist (or his board representative) can be invaluable to the entrepreneur in helping spot potential weaknesses in the management structure, in briefing 'head-hunters' and in joining the recruitment process. An industrially experienced venture capitalist will also be able to act as mediator when strains appear in the management structure. Such intervention may be essential where the business is run by an entrepreneurial partnership whose members eventually become incompatible. Here, the venture capitalist or his representative may even take the chairmanship, at least partly to protect the fund's investment.

Finance

The area where 'hands-on' and 'reactive' venture capital styles meet is on the territory of financial planning and control. Even where the entrepreneur has a financial adviser or controller, the venture capitalist has a 'financial custodianship' role to play. Basically, this role is to ensure that two key mechanisms exist in effective form, namely:

(a) the provision of reliable information about the actual performance of the business and its constituent functions, i.e. research/development, production, and marketing/sales;
(b) the projection and interpretation of such management information to ensure that the inevitable crises which occur are well signposted

and that contingency plans exist to resolve them; also, to ensure that provision is made to cover the penalties of success, without which the business may overtrade – resulting in another kind of disaster.

The venture capitalist and his back-up team will continuously monitor the business's performance, and in effect 'ride herd' on the entrepreneur and his finance director. Where satisfactory financial controls do not exist, the venture capitalist will negotiate with the entrepreneur for a strengthening of the financial function and possibly also for a change of auditors.

Areas of particular sensitivity will be product and process costings, pricing tactics (especially discount structures), capital expenditure evaluation and working capital controls. A computer-driven financial model may well demonstrate the quantitative parameters of each of these, but only an involved investor will be able to interpret their implications for the business. A 'hands-off' style will not give a fund which practises that approach any ability to sense these business dynamics or judge their importance.

Staffing a hands-on fund

As will be apparent, to operate a hands-on style effectively requires a degree of management experience in the venture capitalist which is not usually found among City men – whether professional accountants, fund managers, merchant bankers or lending bankers. Hands-on style funds in the United Kingdom are staffed by a mix of people with solid industrial management experience (often with technical backgrounds), and financially numerate people from the accounting profession or from business schools.

Some funds have recruited manager-technologists from the industrial sector(s) in which they seek to specialise. This practice carries the advantages of in-depth knowledge of a particular technology and will enhance the venture capitalist's personal credibility with the high-tech entrepreneur. A less-well-recognised disadvantage may be that the pace of change is so fast in many of today's and tomorrow's technologies that the manager-technologist rapidly becomes out of date. He will, however, retain a familiarity with the jargon and a knowledge of the basic elements and current trends in his specialisation. He will also know where to go for up-to-date information about developments since his own period of total immersion in the field. All in all, it is probably essential for a serious high-tech fund to employ mainly manager-technologists, with a sprinkling of seasoned venture capitalists.

A variation on this largely in-house expertise is for a small core group of experienced venture capitalists to build a network of external scientific or technological advisers who are full-time academics and industry researchers. This style of operation enables the fund to retain the maximum flexibility while being fully aware of current developments in its chosen investment sectors or technical specialisations. These usually eminent advisers are likely to be on a retainer footing as consultants and will probably be contracted to a single fund, so that the fund can maintain a competitive edge. Such a compromise arrangement is frequently practised by funds which are broad-based and not exclusively high-tech. It is also common, however, for high-tech funds to employ both internal manager-technologists and have access to an outer ring of practising scientists in universities and research bodies.

An interesting North American venture capital practice, which shows signs of developing in the United Kingdom, is that of setting up 'feeder funds', discussed in Chapter 3.

Yet another version of hands-on management, particularly in high-tech investments, is the R & D partnership approach. Here a project originating in a research institute, university or industrial company's R & D facility is mated with a venture capital fund, or funds, with an entrepreneur or business manager. The venture capitalist's skill here is to 'hold the ring' between the originators of the project and the exploiters, while providing the bulk of the finance. At present, initiatives are under way in the United Kingdom to establish such R & D partnerships as an effective form of venture capital – which they have become in the United States. In this case, the hands-on management skills clearly rest with the entrepreneur/business manager, supported by the venture capitalist, while technological input remains with the R & D originators.

Reactive funds

These funds are generally staffed by financially qualified people, e.g. accountants or business graduates. Sometimes they will include industrially experienced managers, but rarely manager-technologists – in contrast with the high-tech hands-on funds.

The style of a *reactive* fund is to be represented on the board of its investee companies, usually by its own staff, but seldom to initiate strategic moves or to assist with technical problem solving. The reactive fund will follow its entrepreneurs, acting as a 'brake' when the financial early warning signs indicate the need, while a *hands-on* fund will actively partner its entrepreneurs in strategic as well as technical matters.

A reactive fund will actively participate in discussions on financial matters, such as capital expenditure, raising new equity finance, acquisitions/disposals and negotiating bank borrowings, leasing, etc. Senior management appointments by the entrepreneurs would also, normally, involve the reactive fund's board representative.

As was indicated in Chapter 7, it is not always easy to draw an exact boundary between a 'reactive' and a 'hands-on' style of venture capital fund. Frequently a fund which is basically reactive will behave as a hands-on fund, for example in early-stage investments and in those where turnaround action is required.

Some apparently reactive funds have adopted a dual-phase style; the fund's own staff do not go on the boards of their investments, but they will appoint carefully selected and experienced industrial managers as their board representatives. These board appointees will not be from the normal genre of non-executive directors. They will frequently have direct experience of the entrepreneur's industrial sector and even of its specific technology; they will be active partners of the entrepreneur, in a capacity best described as 'shadow' or 'guru'. Often they will be successful entrepreneurs themselves, senior managers in larger companies, or early-retired board-level executives from the same or neighbouring industries. How should such a fund be categorised – hands-on or reactive? Hard and fast categories are not easy to define in the venture capital industry.

Hands-off or passive funds

The key characteristic of both *hands-on* and *reactive* funds is that they are, in differing degrees, active venture capitalists. A *hands-off* fund is, by contrast, a passive investor, where contact with the entrepreneur is infrequent and usually at his initiative rather than the fund's. Board representation is rare among hands-off funds, although the fund may reserve the right to appoint a director. It is frequently the case that a hands-off fund will receive only semi-annual or statutory annual financial information, compared with monthly or even weekly information as will be the case with most hands-on and reactive funds.

The hands-off fund will play little or no part in discussing and formulating strategy with the entrepreneur, or in sanctioning capital expenditure or management appointments. It will, however, usually have various pre-emption rights regarding the raising of new equity or share transfers, as well as placing limitations on overall borrowings. Commentators on the industry frequently ask whether hands-off funds are really venture capitalists rather than traditional investors in un-listed investments. A number of these passive or hands-off funds specialise as followers of investment syndicates, where the leader is a hands-on or at least reactive fund.

To confuse the issue further, a hands-on or reactive fund may occasionally invest in a hands-off style! Perhaps it is a syndicate member in a buy-out or later-stage expansion financing of a well-managed business with a proven profits record, or it may be investing as junior partner in a two- or three-fund syndicate where it has no directly

Table 7. Causes of business failure: the A-score short list

Defects	
Autocratic chief executive	8
Chairman and chief executive combined	4
Passive board	2
Unbalanced skills, especially over-technical	2
Weak finance director	2
Poor management depth below board level	1
No budgetary control	3
No cash flow plans, or no cash flow updating	3
No reliable costing system	3
Poor response to change, unawareness of business environment	15
Total for Defects	43
Danger mark for Defects	10
Mistakes	
High debt gearing	15
Overtrading (inadequate equity base)	15
Big project in relation to business size	15
Total for Mistakes	45
Danger mark for Mistakes	15
Symptoms	
Financial signs, e.g. Z-score warning signs	4
Creative accounting, especially changes to previous policy resulting in increased stock values, lower depreciation, and capitalisation of R & D or repairs/maintenance	4
Non-financial signs, including deterioration in product quality/service, premises and morale	3
Terminal signs	1
Total for Symptoms	12
Total Overall maximum possible	100
Danger mark Overall	25

applicable industrial or technological expertise among its own staff. The potential upside may be too tempting to miss in that the likely rewards may excite the hands-on fund sufficiently for it to forgo its normal mode of active aftercare.

Causes of business failure

Much has been written about identifying business failure in advance of its arrival, particularly with the use of mathematical ratios such as the Z-score. What has not yet been covered in depth are the prime *causes* of failure in venture capital investments in particular. Work on this subject owes much to John Argenti, who has devised the A-score as a non-statistical means of attributing the causes of business failure. Table 7 shows the A-score short list, which results in a points score for each business. For any business to score over 25 means danger, particularly if the score in the 'Mistakes' section is also 10 or more.

11 Exits

The open and fundamental objective of a true venture capitalist, when investing, is eventually to realise his investment at a substantial capital profit. His investment timescale to realisation (as we saw in Chapter 3) can be anything from two or three years to as much as ten years. In certain cases, the venture capitalist may not realise all his original holding – particularly where a stock market, USM or OTC quotation is involved and where he judges that further capital growth is likely.

There are a number of voluntary exits for a capital realisation. It must not be forgotten that involuntary exits are often achieved in venture capital through receivership or liquidation of failed investments. Sometimes a voluntary exit is sought as the only alternative to failure. In these cases there is likely to be a loss on the cost of investment, though not as great as it would be if receivership or liquidation followed.

Voluntary realisations are arrived at from one of three basic exit routes:

(a) A trade sale to another industrial company.
(b) A repurchase of the venture capitalist's shares by the entrepreneur, or directly by his company.
(c) A share quotation, through a full stock market listing, a USM (Unlisted Securities Market) quote or an OTC (over-the-counter) quote.

Before realisation can be achieved, there are several pre-conditions to be fulfilled.

Pre-conditions for realisation

Whichever exit route is followed, adjustments must usually be made to the company's capital structure as well as to the arrangements between the venture capitalist and the investee company or its entrepreneur.

The deal structures at the different rounds of financing will probably have brought in equity elements other than ordinary shares – notably preferred ordinary, preference shares and even convertible loan stock. Before full or even partial realisation can take place, most of these elements will require redemption or repayment if they are not convertible. If convertible, then conversion will occur before realisation, allowing the venture capitalist to enter his full equity entitlement. Any special forms of debt instrument provided by the venture capitalist will normally be repayable on a sale or quotation, or change of control. There are sometimes complex negotiations between investors and entrepreneur to establish an agreed valuation of these non-ordinary share instruments, especially where preferred income or profits participation rights apply.

It may be necessary for the venture capitalist's board nominee to retire or resign, even though he is a non-executive director. Where the nominee is an independent, with knowledge of the industrial sector or relevant technology, it is likely to be beneficial – in a stock market, USM or OTC quotation – for him to remain with the company. Where he is a member of the venture capitalist's management team, it is usually inappropriate for him to continue as a non-executive director. If the realisation is through a trade sale or repurchase of shares by the investee company, then it is probable that any nominee of the venture capital fund would retire or resign.

Similarly, any special rights of approval or veto by the venture capitalist(s) which were agreed with the entrepreneur at the time of investment (see Chapter 9) will usually be eliminated, whichever the exit route.

Trade sale

Despite the considerable publicity for the USM since it was formed in 1980, most exits are still achieved through sale of the company to another business.

Normally, the initiative in a trade sale rests with the potential acquirer, who will be interested in the acquisition for a variety of reasons – each of which can apply to any acquisition, whether of a young business or of a well-established mature business, quoted or not.

It is likely that a young, high-technology business which is acquired will fill a key niche in the acquirer's product line or will bring some important technological contribution to the acquiring business. Equally, the entrepreneur may be highly satisfied to 'cash in his chips' without developing the business further so that it can achieve a share quotation under its own power. Usually, surprising though it may seem, a trade sale will actually bring a higher valuation to the entrepreneur with a *sound* business (and to his venture capitalist) than does a USM, OTC or full stock market quotation.

The reason for this is basically the certainty in the acquirer's mind of the contribution which is likely to be made to his business by the proposed acquisition. On a share quotation, however, the new passive investors are unlikely to be expert in the business and will be swayed more by the current fashion appeal of the industrial sector in which the entrepreneur's business operates. In other words, USM, OTC or stock market investors do not always discriminate as to the quality of the business offered provided it is in the 'right sector'. It is, therefore, possible for a *modest* business in a favoured sector to achieve a higher exit valuation than would be gained on a trade sale.

Frequently on a trade sale, the acquiring company will seek a net assets warranty, and possibly an underwritten profits guarantee. There may be an adjustment to the consideration in either direction, dependent upon profits achieved in the current and/or subsequent year(s).

Share repurchase

As a less 'final' exit route than a trade sale, and as an alternative to share quotation, it is now possible (Companies Act 1981) for a company to buy back its own shares from its venture capitalists or from any other shareholder. Previously it was possible, exceptionally, to issue and redeem certain classes of preferred or preference shares (Companies Act 1948, Section 58), but there were stringent rules concerning the maintaining of the capital base by the issue of further shares or by the transfer of profits to a non-distributable reserve (or sinking fund) for redemption purposes.

The 1981 Companies Act extended this facility to allow the purchase of a company's own shares and the issue of redeemable shares of any class. The main conditions of a share repurchase are as follows:

(a) The company must have some non-redeemable shares in issue.
(b) The share purchase can be made out of distributable reserves (or profits) or out of the proceeds of a new issue of shares.
(c) If, and only if, the distributable reserves and new issue proceeds

options are exhausted, the repurchase or redemption can be made out of capital (but the directors must make an audited statutory declaration of solvency, and a special resolution is required).

(d) The shares being redeemed or repurchased must have been owned for at least five years, although there are specific circumstances where the period can be reduced to three years.

The actual process requires advance clearance from the Inland Revenue, and there are other technical points which make the advice of experienced professional accountants essential.

The buy-back of shares from a venture capitalist(s) is usually provided for by a two-way option negotiated at the outset of the investment, to be triggered after a period of years or on some pre-agreed profits (or net assets) threshold being reached, if a share quotation has not been achieved. The entrepreneur may prefer this option to a share quotation for a variety of reasons:

(a) He may not wish to 'go public', even through the USM or OTC, with the often-quoted disadvantages of the public spotlight, the short-term performance yardstick and the lack of freedom in his running of the company.

(b) The business may be in a sector which is out of fashion among investors; thus he may not reach an adequate valuation for his business (in his view).

(c) The performance of the business may not be sufficiently sparkling to attract a stockbroking or merchant banking sponsor for the listing.

Most venture capital funds will currently agree to a buy-back option being incorporated in the original investment documentation at the time of investment. Where such an option does not exist, it can sometimes be negotiated.

If the company does not meet the Companies Act requirements for a buy-back, or if there is unlikely to be sufficient cash available from the company's own resources, then it is always technically possible for the entrepreneur personally to buy out the venture capitalist, provided he can raise the cash required.

The popularity of buy-back is unlikely to become established for some time because the legislation has permitted these arrangements only since 1981, and a buy-back option will usually become 'live' only after several years. The legislation stipulates a minimum of five years, in any case.

Many unlisted companies that have venture capitalists seeking an exit within the usual maximum timescale of 7–10 years may provide this exit through a buy-back mechanism. Despite the present USM attractions of high share ratings (which may not continue), the British entrepreneur has a greater love of privacy than his North American counterpart. Thus for his own realisation to be achieved, he may want to remain unlisted until a trade sale possibility arrives.

Public share quotation

Much has been written on the subject of the stock market and its recent protégé, the Unlisted Securities Market (USM). Less is generally known about the as yet smaller over-the-counter market (OTC), which manifests itself in various forms, including that of Granville & Co. (formerly M. J. H. Nightingale & Co.). An overview of each of these exits is given here with a firm rider that specialist financial advice from experienced professionals (merchant banks, accountants, commercial lawyers or stockbrokers) is required before a company commits itself to any one of them.

Why go public?

The arguments for and against a public share quotation are, briefly, as follows:

For

(a) Improves marketability of owners' shares and independent valuation of these.
(b) Shares can be issued to raise new funds, or as consideration for acquisitions.
(c) A company's status is enhanced in both its industry and its markets.
(d) Employees can benefit from 'real' share incentive schemes.

Against

(a) Disclosure requirement demanding, and management freedom of action limited.
(b) Emphasis by investors on short-term profits and dividends performance, at possible risk to long-term plans of company.
(c) Directors' benefits restricted, and higher share valuations have Capital Transfer Tax (CTT) effects.
(d) High once-off costs of quotation, whether full listing or USM.

Full listing versus USM?

For a small but growing company with venture capital support, the USM has most of the benefits of the fully listed market, plus some special advantages with few perceivable disadvantages, after more than four years' experience to date. While all the advantages of a public market are maintained, there is a lower level of external scrutiny and involvement; pressure for dividends is also less likely since USM companies are generally regarded by investors as capital growth prospects rather than income-yielding investments. Indeed, the price/earnings multiples of USM companies are generally higher than their fully listed 'bigger brothers'.

Further, special advantages over a full listing include the following:

(a) Only a three-year (or, exceptionally, shorter) trading record is necessary, compared with a mandatory five-year minimum.
(b) A minimum of only 10% of the issued ordinary share capital has to be listed, compared with 25%.
(c) An accountants' report and working capital 'comfort' letter are not mandatory (but the sponsor may require these).
(d) Up to now, new listings on the USM are possible at a higher entry valuation than is achievable on the fully listed market.
(e) The quotation costs are substantially less at about £100,000 as compared with about £250,000.
(f) Share valuations are reduced by 20–50% for CTT purposes.
(g) After listing, there is far greater freedom for USM companies to carry out large capital transactions without accountants' reports or shareholder approval (not necessarily a good thing, but undoubtedly an attraction).

The USM, founded in November 1980, developed from Rule 163, under which The Stock Exchange had allowed, since the early 1950s, buyers and sellers of shares to be matched – where few bargains were made and the volume of trading was low.

It was always envisaged by The Stock Exchange that the USM would provide a transitional or 'nursery' staging post for companies *en route* to a full listing. The transition is cheap and relatively simple, and the documentation can be minimal, depending on whether a full prospectus – including an accountants' report – was issued at the time of USM entry.

There are no firm rules about how long a company should remain on the USM before it 'graduates' to the full market. Pressure may be brought if the percentage of equity traded increases towards the 50% level, or if the total market capitalisation of the company concerned is out of balance with the other USM stocks, e.g. at over £100 million currently. For the purpose of spotting 'promotion candidates', The Stock Exchange reviews the USM companies annually on an informal basis. Some 10% of USM companies have graduated to a full listing.

The methods of USM entry are similar to those applying to the fully listed market, namely a *placing*, an *offer for sale*, a *tender* or an *introduction*.

Placing. This, the most usual method, is where the shares are offered to clients of the sponsors, both to private individuals and to institutions. The Stock Exchange insists that 25% of all such 'placing' shares be offered to jobbers so the general public can subscribe and thus ensure an adequate 'after market'.

There is a maximum size limit on the prospective valuation of a company at time of placing – currently £15 million – before an offer for sale is necessary. The maximum size of the placing itself is currently £3 million.

A placing costs 5–15% of the monetary value of the shares being placed, total costs typically falling in the range of £50,000–£100,000. This includes a small (usually 0.5%) underwriting commission to the issue's sponsors.

Offer for sale. This method involves the issue of a prospectus, inviting subscriptions from the general public at a fixed price. The sponsor will arrange an underwriting consortium, which is committed to taking up any shares not accepted in the market.

An offer for sale costs more than a placing, largely due to the required advertising (e.g. three pages in the *Financial Times*); the underwriting commission is in the range 1¼–2%. Total costs are thus about double those incurred in a placing.

Tender offer. This takes the same form as an offer for sale, except that the issue price is not fixed. Investors are invited to bid at prices in excess of a defined minimum, and the final 'striking' price is the minimum at which all the shares being offered can be sold. The costs of a tender offer are similar to those of an offer for sale.

Introduction. When a company already has a spread of shareholders and is not raising any new capital, The Stock Exchange will allow this form of entry to the USM. This is a low-cost method of quotation and is used where there was a private placing of shares, usually with institutions, before the USM entry. An introduction can also be used when a company is graduating from the 'Rule 163' market, which provided most of the early USM entrants. Rule 163 is now used only for dealings in companies where there are infrequent bargins. It is no longer a source of many USM entrants.

The USM is already showing evidence of becoming an attractive exit for venture capitalists in countries outside the United Kingdom. There are now USM quotations for French, Dutch, Swedish, Norwegian and Danish companies. It is probable that this feature will grow, since the USM can fulfil a similar role for the smaller UK and, indeed, European companies, as do the US over-the-counter markets for the smaller US and Canadian companies. In fact, the USM was designed to resemble closely the US OTC, which the UK OTC versions do not approach in either activity or status.

It must be emphasised that the USM is not yet a mature, stable market. Cases of exaggerated promise on USM entry are beginning to emerge, and it is widely expected that the heady premium valuations on the USM will eventually adjust downwards to equate more closely to those of the fully listed market. The Stock Exchange insists that each USM prospectus carries a 'danger to your health' warning to the prospective investor!

Over-the-counter markets (OTC)

The OTC market in the United Kingdom was launched in 1972 by Granville & Co. (formerly M. J. H. Nightingale & Co.) as an innovation in the equity financing spectrum. The objective was to provide unlisted companies with an alternative to the fully listed market by introducing them to investing institutions and making a 'matched bargain' market in their shares. In the decade since the first OTC market, over 30 companies' shares have been traded in by more than 60 institutional and 3,000 private investors.

The advent of the USM has undoubtedly led to many potential OTC candidates choosing the former. This is largely for reasons of more attractive initial valuations and the official stamp of approval bestowed on the USM by The Stock Exchange. There are, however, signs that both Granville's and the newer OTC market launched in 1982 by several smaller stockbrokers will become increasingly attractive.

The various forms of OTC have common elements. None of them are officially blessed by The Stock Exchange, all operate on the basis of matched buyers and sellers, and none have the rigour of The Stock Exchange rules applied to the fully listed market and USM. Granville's OTC does, however, claim to follow The Stock Exchange's listing agreement and is likely to be more demanding than other OTCs –

which represent an effort to develop a third tier, below the USM, to the 'senior' market.

For a company seeking an OTC exit, there will be many of the USM's advantages without some of its restrictions; but the market in their shares is not likely to be as active (nor as volatile) as either the USM or the full market. Nor will any OTC quotation carry the same prestige as a quotation on either the USM or the full market.

Basically, the Granville OTC investor is likely to be more interested in medium-to-long-term capital gains than in the short-term-dealing gains that can arise from the rapid price movements in the USM and fully listed market. The stockbroker-led OTC market is not yet clearly established as a firm fixture in the share markets and has not yet become as favoured among the major institutions as is Granville & Co.

The costs of an OTC quotation are lower than the equivalent USM or full listing, but there is no discount for an OTC company that decides at a later date to transfer to either the USM or full market – whereas a USM company can usually transfer to the full market at a modest cost increment.

Part four Some key issues

Introduction

The UK venture capital industry is young, dynamic and growing fast. While the UK practitioner can look across the Atlantic for guidance as to the pitfalls and hurdles he will inevitably face, it is a mistake to assume US experience can be transplanted directly to Europe in general and into the United Kingdom in particular. The European entrepreneur is not a carbon copy of his transatlantic cousin, and the fiscal and related legislative regimes in Europe are basically more hostile to the smaller business than in the United States. Despite the very real strides which have been made since 1980 in the United Kingdom especially, the US Small Business Administration and its SBICs (Small Business Investment Companies) have no equal yet in Europe, nor does there seem to be any prospect of a similar initiative.

Above all, no European market offers the same scale of potential growth to its entrepreneurs as does the US market to its own. The European Economic Community has been 'in business' for a quarter century, but there is no sign as yet of a homogeneous market among the EEC's 270 million consumers, which is greater than the 230 million of the United States.

In this section, a number of issues are covered which are important to the future health and progress of the UK venture capital industry. Some of the thoughts expressed, which are entirely personal, may be controversial. This is not intentional, but venture capitalists in the United Kingdom do not always share a common view on the issues, which may thus benefit from an airing. The issues covered are the following:

(a) Entrepreneurship in the United Kingdom (Chapter 12), including cultural handicaps, fiscal handicaps, and equity, debt and control.
(b) Fund management styles and stamina (Chapter 13), including

discussion of high-technology funds, deal flow and venture capital funds taxation.

(c) The role of the State (Chapter 14).

Chapter 15, Continental Europe, provides a summary of current venture capital activity across the EEC.

12 Entrepreneurship in the United Kingdom

Why has the UK venture capital industry taken so long to develop, compared with the United States? Why do small firms in the United States make a substantially greater contribution to economic growth and new employment than is the UK experience?

The US venture capital industry really began to gather momentum after 1950. It was fuelled in those early days by private wealth, through individuals and their charitable foundations, followed by large corporations; institutional investors were notably absent. Many of those private foundations and large corporations were started by entrepreneurs during the present century. The concept of 'old wealth' begetting 'new wealth' through successive generations of entrepreneurs seeking initial backing from the successful entrepreneurs of previous generations has been the backbone of the US experience – strongly abetted, of course, by the almost universal business orientation of US culture.

UK cultural handicaps

The UK was the cradle of modern entrepreneurism from the seventeenth century, and throughout the next 200 years and more, British entrepreneurs led the world. The Industrial Revolution in the late 1700s and early 1800s was founded around such names as Watt, Stephenson, Brunel, Wilkinson, Ramsden, Naysmith, Symington, Arkwright and Hargreaves. A number of British entrepreneurs also led the way in establishing continental European ventures – notably Humphrey Edwards (the Chaillot engineering plant in France), W. T. Mulvaney (Ruhr expansion projects) and Richard Roberts (the Koechlin cotton mill at Mulhouse). These men were the engineering forerunners of today's Silicon Valley computer science entrepreneurs. Why did the United Kingdom lose this world lead in entrepreneurism to the United States from the early 1900s? Can it catch up? How can this gap be closed?

Social barriers

When the United Kingdom's early entrepreneurs sought financial backing, their principal source was the 'old wealth' of the landed gentry, including the family aristocracies of many generations' vintage. Perhaps naturally, when these entrepreneurs became financially successful in their own right, they began to adopt the habits and prejudices of the 'old wealth'. Although the latter was willing to invest in 'trade and manufacture', it rarely became involved directly. Its education was in the arts and classics, its wealth in the land; its children went into the professions, the City or the church.

The social unpopularity of industry and trade as a career stemmed from the mid-nineteenth century, and it is still evident today, 100 years later. Many self-made men of the 1970s and 1980s are still adopting the life-styles of the 'old wealth', including the habit of guiding their own children into the professions (the civil service, accountancy, medicine and law) or the City. Few successful industrialists today encourage their children to train for a career in industry.

Educational barriers

Largely because of the way in which today's educational system has developed from the early 1900s, discrimination against industry remains within the school curricula. Science is taught as a pure, academic subject, rather than as a practical, application-orientated discipline. The field of mathematics is notoriously short of experienced teachers. The arts and social sciences, including economics, continue to be the favoured subjects, just as they have been for the past century and more.

An additional penalty suffered by industry at the education stage is the post-war anti-trade prejudice in the teaching profession, resulting, unfortunately, from old-fashioned ideas about the industrialist as the exploiter and the industrial employee as the exploited. Teachers today rarely encourage their students to consider a career in industry rather than in the academic, professional or educational fields.

There are early signs that change may be on the way, particularly with the recent introduction of computers into school life. However, it will take at least a decade before the attitude of all teaching can be reorientated and students actively persuaded to consider an industrial career. Of particular interest is the TVEI project in Birmingham (Technical and Vocational Education Initiative), aimed at secondary school curricula, to bring industry and education together. The scheme has the support of the Manpower Services Commission, the Confederation of British Industry and the central Government's Department of Education.

Employment security

Until the 1980 recession, post-war employment in the United Kingdom was something of a sinecure in most industries. The Welfare State had looked after the employee and his dependants, literally from cradle to grave. For more than 30 years, income had been heavily taxed to sustain the Welfare State's generosity. Job mobility was not favoured, and to have spent a whole career with one employer – a Victorian virtue – was still widely respected. Pensions were designed to penalise heavily the early leaver and to lock in the senior executive ranks.

In this environment of all-round job security, people did not take career risks voluntarily. The incentives to start their own businesses were not great, largely due to a consistent neglect of the small-business sector by successive governments. 'Big' was 'beautiful', and the agglomeration of large groups was encouraged. Share incentive schemes for executives were specifically penalised except during a brief period in the later 1960s and early 1970s. Not surprisingly, small-business entrepreneurship lay largely fallow.

The 1980s: a turning point?

Conventional wisdom has it that the entrepreneurial flair of British society, so fundamental to the pre-eminence of the United Kingdom as the world's leading industrial nation throughout the 1700s and 1800s, has too long been smothered by egalitarian politics during the 1900s. Until the recent deep recession, which lasted more than three years, this was evident. Increasingly, however, signs of a new entrepreneurial spirit have begun to show, encouraging the belief that the United Kingdom can once again generate its own entrepreneurism. This is partly due to the new realities resulting from the failure of large companies to maintain employment during the recession, leading to many skilled and able people being made redundant and to many 30–50-year-old executives seeing their future promotion paths blocked due to lack of growth in their organisations.

Never have so many new businesses been formed as in the years of the early 1980s. A breed of small businessmen is emerging, who have been trained in the larger groups and thus have modern business management disciplines to add to the entrepreneur's basic weaponry of ideas, drive and enthusiasm. This new and most promising generation of entrepreneurs is being encouraged in many ways by a wide range of Government measures aimed specifically at the small-business sector (see Chapter 14). There is also an unprecedented amount of funding available for the small businessman.

An important handicap which remains is the continuing social resistance to acknowledging trade and industry as a 'top of the ladder' slot in society, alongside doctors, lawyers, accountants, scientists and civil servants. This handicap extends through to the educational barriers already discussed.

Undoubtedly, the achieved and publicly perceived personal and corporate successes of the new wave of entrepreneurs will gradually break down these important barriers, thus underpinning the new entrepreneurial revolution. Public recognition given to industry through the honours system, which has begun to include successful small-business entrepreneurs, will also help. However, distaste for the profit motive dies hard and is still far too evident among many 'levellers' in British society.

No such problem exists in the United States, where nearly everyone knows a self-made millionaire from his own home town and is driven to emulate rather than envy or distrust his example. It would thus be a mistake to expect UK entrepreneurism to match that of the United States too soon, if ever. Fundamental changes in British society must occur first.

Fiscal handicaps: executive share options

The course of most venture capital investments is hazardous. One of the key ingredients for success in taking a company from its early stages of seed capital or start-up to a flourishing, expanding, medium-sized concern is the ability of the original management to develop from clever entrepreneurs into rounded business managers. In the United States, the cradle of the modern venture capital system, most venture capital investments are headed by one or two men who embrace these qualities of technical entrepreneurship and disciplined business management skills.

In the United Kingdom, by contrast, at this stage in the development of the venture capital industry, there is evidence that the original entrepreneurs frequently have not had business management experience of the kind which will equip them to expand their businesses by relying solely upon their original team. Where these entrepreneurs are sired by the larger companies with well-regarded business management disciplines (especially US subsidiaries in the United Kingdom and the latter's own advanced technology companies), it is possible to find the successful US-style combination of the original entrepreneur. More frequently, however, the hands-on venture capitalist finds he must attract into the entrepreneur's team at least one high-calibre experienced manager from outside the business, in order to safeguard and successfully realise the growth potential which led the venture capitalist to back the entrepreneur in the first place.

Executives of the right stature and experience in larger companies are likely to be aged 35 to 55, highly rewarded in terms of salary, pension and perks, and will have a degree of security in their employment which is clearly not possible in an emerging small company. Neither will that small company be able to match the salary and pension levels available from the executive's current employers.

In the United States one of the key ingredients in the success of the venture capital industry has been the ability of the transferring executive to bring with him a pot of savings from his high salary (with low income tax rates) in order to buy a piece of the equity. The practice of granting executive share options to the transferring executive, on which he pays only capital gains tax, is also normal in North America.

For the UK venture capitalist to bridge this fundamental problem has been doubly difficult. First, the senior executive has seen his high salary suffer high income tax, with the result that he does not have a pot of savings with which to buy a piece of the equity in the smaller business – to motivate him adequately or to tempt him to move into this low-security, high-risk area. Second, under the tax legislation in the UK (until June 1984), any share options granted to such an executive were subject to income tax, both on share realisation and, more seriously, on any uplift in the notional value of the option shares before realisation.

Provisions were introduced from 6 April 1984 whereby companies may, with Inland Revenue approval, establish schemes to provide employees and directors with options to acquire shares in their employer, a company which controls their employer, or certain companies which have an interest in it through a consortium. In contrast to the treatment of unapproved schemes, there will be no income tax charge on the exercise of the option or on the sale of the shares acquired, the only charge to tax being the normal capital gains tax liability on the disposal of the shares. An income tax charge may, however, arise on the grant of an option to purchase shares at less than their market value (although any 'manifest discount' to market value will, in any case, normally prevent the scheme from obtaining approval). There is a limit on the value (at the time of grant) of the shares over which an individual may hold options, i.e. the greater of £100,000 or four times his emoluments for the current or previous year. In order to obtain the full benefit of the exemptions available the employee must not exercise options earlier than three years, or later than ten years, after the grant, nor more frequently than once every three years.

Equity, debt and control

In early-stage financings, for businesses at the seed, start-up or even second-round phase of development, deal structuring is particularly difficult. The asset base is small, or may have been eliminated altogether through the business's early trading losses. The entrepreneur has exhausted his own resources, which provided the original asset base, and he has usually borrowed against personal security – notably his own house.

Over-borrowing

Despite the almost total risk taken by the entrepreneur, a bank is not usually prepared to do more than match an entrepreneur's own commitment, whatever the security arrangements. Thus an equity contribution of £25,000 by the entrepreneur may bring an additional £25,000 of borrowings. It is likely that in the first year or two the business will incur losses. These losses reduce the original equity base; a £25,000 loss in year one followed by the same in year two would mean a deficit in shareholders' funds of £25,000 – a recurring scenario, even if the exact numbers vary. The lending base is first eliminated, then becomes a negative amount equal to the original lending. This is an alarming state of affairs for the lender, who will often subsequently require repayment of the original £25,000.

The business may reach break-even point at £200,000 sales. With a working capital ratio of 25% (stocks and trade debtors less trade creditors) it will require a further £50,000 of cash to meet such a sales target. The bank is unlikely to lend more, and so an external injection of equity is required. If this injection is £50,000 it will merely bring existing borrowings at £25,000 into line with the new equity base of £25,000 (£25,000 deficit plus £50,000 injection = new equity base of

£25,000). To go forward is difficult, and the entrepreneur may have to suffer loss of control of his business to the new equity providers. An equity injection at the outset – even of the same £25,000 as provided through borrowings – would probably have had no servicing cost initially (compared with at least 10% cost if through borrowings) and might well have prevented such a situation from occuring, provided the entrepreneur was prepared to surrender equity at that stage.

Figure 2 demonstrates this state of affairs. The figures used are purely illustrative, although the circumstances are all too frequent in the experience of many accountants and other small business advisers.

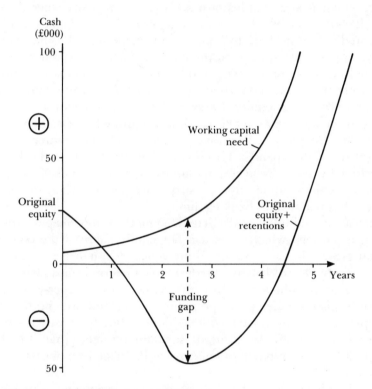

Fig. 2 Early-stage financing: equity *v.* debt
Start: Equity = £25,000; initial borrowings £25,000.
Year two: Funding gap = £75,000.
            Equity/borrowing base = negative £25,000.
            Borrowing capacity = negative, but borrowings £25,000.
            Minimum equity injection = £50,000 → 100% gearing and equity dilution to 33% for original shareholders.
This chart is derived from work by Brian Warnes, Managing Director of Midland Bank Venture Capital and author of *The Genghis Khan Guide to Business* (Osmosis Publications, 1984), in which the graph appears as 'The Death Valley Curve'.

Entrepreneur resistance: the equity dilution syndrome

Just the recipe for an equity injection from a venture capitalist? Yes, as long as the entrepreneur is ready to surrender equity control, or the venture capitalist is prepared to overvalue the entrepreneur's equity to avoid having control.

The UK entrepreneur has traditionally resisted 'giving' any meaningful equity to outsiders. This has been one of the more recognised and less discussed reasons for the lack of a progressively developing small-business sector in the United Kingdom. The British entrepreneur has limited his business's growth to a size where he still has full control. He will have borrowed as much as the bank will allow, and usually then sits back to enjoy a comfortable small-business life.

Any opportunity to expand the business further – whether organically or by acquisition – is measured first against whether he can borrow more from the bank, and second against whether he can retain ownership of 100% of his equity. Rarely will the entrepreneur accept new equity from outside to make possible the growth decision, without which the company will always remain small. The entrepreneur's natural drive to expand a business is thus tempered, in the United Kingdom, by his desire to keep undiluted his absolute mastery over the business. This attitude often persists, surprisingly, when the entrepreneur has reached his banking 'limits'.

Such an attitude often makes it difficult for the venture capital fund to design a package which gives it a fair equity share of the potential capital growth in the business. Some venture capitalists may be prepared to provide an element of redeemable preferred shares which are non-voting but which will carry a compensatory 'super-yield' and probably also a redemption premium. The result will be that the entrepreneur minimises his equity dilution, but his business profitability and cash flow will concede substantially more than if he had accepted a higher initial dilution. Annexe 1C (page 180) illustrates this effect.

A variation which may be acceptable to the entrepreneur is that of an 'earn-out' structure. Here, the initial dilution is limited and the venture capitalist's valuation is based on a realistic multiple of prospective profits. If these profits are achieved, the equity dilution remains as at the outset. If, however, a lower profits figure is achieved – over one, two, three or more years – then the dilution is greater, with the venture capitalist having an increased shareholding. In the United Kingdom, the 'earn-out' concept is not yet widely accepted among entrepreneurs.

In the United States in general and in many UK management buy-outs, the earn-out is a standard technique in venture capitalism. Annexe 3A (page 187) refers to this method of deal structuring.

The alternative is for the venture capitalist to attribute an over-generous valuation to the business at its current stage of development. This may appeal to the entrepreneur, but is not to be advised if the venture capitalist has to achieve competitive performance returns in his own activity. Regrettably, there are funds which may not have such clear performance objectives and which are prepared to bid up equity values – thus achieving a comparably lower share of the equity, acceptable to the entrepreneur. Despite such apparent flexibility, many venture capital deals are not consummated because of the 'equity dilution syndrome', and consequently many small businesses with real growth potential are destined to remain small.

Venture capitalists' resistance: the small-ticket equity problem

Even if the British entrepreneur readily accepted equity dilution for the benefit of a larger business, few venture capitalists are prepared to invest the small amounts of equity needed at the early stages of business development. To provide sums below £150–200,000 requires the same due diligence process as with amounts two or three times larger, in terms of investigation and aftercare. Paradoxically, often greater care is needed prior to investment because of the unproved nature of the product, the process and the entrepreneur himself.

The argument runs something like the following: the fund's man-agement overhead cannot be rewarded adequately from the potential income yield on an equity investment of, say, £100,000. The only possible recompense is the eventual capital gain, but the ability of the venture capitalist to make confident judgements about the real growth potential in small-scale, early-stage, as yet unprofitable businesses is far more uncertain than for businessses which are established and already in profit. The risks of investing £250,000 or more – the usual starting point for most UK venture capital funds – may be nearly as great, but the size of investment justifies the scale of investigation and aftercare involved.

Clearly, such an equity financing gap exists in the £25,000 to £200,000 investment range. For many decades, a similar size gap persisted in the long-term borrowing needs of smaller businesses, and ICFC's birth in 1947 was largely conceived to fill this lending gap. Some attempts have been made by captive funds to fill the equivalent equity gap, usually bank-related funds or offshoots of the semi-State venture capital organisations, but it is probably fair to say that these rare and laudable attempts are not always seen as wholly profit-related and totally commercial in their objectives.

With the advent of the State-sponsored Loan Guarantee Scheme (LGS) and the Business Start-up Scheme (BSS) in 1980, there now appear to be enabling instruments to provide quasi-equity to fill this gap. Unfortunately, the LGS is still debt, not equity, and the BSS has given way to the BES, which favours investment in established rather than new businesses, and in amounts usually greater than £150,000 – for the same reasons of economy of management overheads as with non-BES venture capital funds.

Can the gap be plugged by other than State-sponsored instruments or by less than wholly commercially inspired initiatives from private-sector institutions? There is evidence from the United States that the Small Business Administration, through the SBICs (Small Business Investment Companies), has enabled local and regional funds to become viable, although professionally staffed, because of their geographical and/or industrial sector limitation – allowing more effective application of their expensive management skills.

Future auguries

In the United Kingdom there are already a few examples, from funds launched in 1983 and 1984, of attempts to focus the expensive management overhead inherent in a professional venture capital fund on small-ticket equity investment. Among these are the Avon Enterprise Fund, based in Bristol and operating in Avon, Somerset, Gloucestershire and Wiltshire; Northern Capital Investors, based in Newcastle; Oakland Management, operating from the Thames Valley; and Darnaway Venture Capital Fund, operating in Scotland.

The *small-ticket equity problem* may thus yet find at least a partial solution as far as the UK venture capitalists' historical reluctance is concerned. With regard to the *equity dilution problem*, the younger generation of entrepreneurs which is now emerging appears much more prepared to concede meaningful equity positions to its backers than was the case prior to the 1980s. There are, as a result, cautious grounds for hope that the serious gap in small-ticket equity may eventually be plugged.

13 Fund management styles and stamina

The successful fund

It remains an open question whether the recent rapid expansion of the UK venture capital industry heralds another false dawn, as in the late 1960s, or whether most of the current 100 or more funds are here to stay as a permanent and valuable part of the United Kingdom's financial infrastructure. A safe prediction is that it is unlikely all of today's funds will survive over the next decade or so.

From observing the development of the US venture capital industry over the past quarter century, it seems clear that the successful venture capital funds will have certain common characteristics, whatever their specialisations – whether classified by technology or by financing stage (start-up, 'mezzanine', buy-out, etc.).

The *first group* of characteristics concerns the successful fund's management team, which will be independent of any other responsibilities, even if part of a larger organisation. It will have a mix of skill in-house rather than relying largely on outside advice and will, above all, include industrial general management experience as well as financial expertise.

Industrial marketing and technical skills are essential in satisfying three key requirements for successful venture capitalists:

(a) The ability, actively, to identify and 'attract' specific potential investments, rather than solely reacting to proposals brought in by intermediaries.
(b) The skill to investigate speedily yet thoroughly business propositions where an adequate factual base is absent and where a calculated risk may or may not be just feasible, often relying on past experience.

(c) The competence to 'add value' to their investments by active, informed advice to and support for the entrepreneurs, particularly by involvement in business strategy formulation and major tactical decisions; and the experience to guide investee managements through their inevitable difficult patches by drawing on the venture capitalist's own management background.

In all the above, technical skills are also important, but the extent to which they are needed in-house depends upon how technologically specialised is the fund's mission. Whatever the individual fund's skills mix, where it is based solely on financial evaluation expertise it will be less likely to succeed in the long term.

The *second group* of characteristics concerns the attitudes of the fund's own investors. A successful fund's backers will share the following:

(a) A willingness to be undemanding towards their venture capital funds throughout the early period after launch. This may last several years, when the backers receive no yield and net asset values are in decline, and with the failures which will certainly occur long before the 'big winners' are realised. At present, it is almost 'fashionable' for institutions to invest in the venture capital industry. Institutions also normally have rather short-term horizons, with their own managers subject to frequent assessment against competitive performance indices. A significant relaxation in this attitude will be required if the recent blossoming of venture capital in the United Kingdom is to be sustained.

(b) An appreciation of the 'step' nature of growth in young businesses, which will almost inevitably require sequential or multiphase financing by the original venture capital fund. In more conventional investments, it is often regarded as a failure if more finance has to be injected before the investee company has proved its success. US experience has taught us that a venture capital fund's 'big winners' rarely emerge before there have been several stages of finance – some while the investee company is still loss-making and cash-hungry. Where the institutional backers have influence over a venture capital fund's investment decisions, they may often have to adopt an approach of blind courage in authorising further tranches of funding into an unproved investment.

(c) A firm encouragement to the fund's management to spread its overall risk through syndication of deals, not always by taking the lead. Syndication in the United States has allowed investment in many more high-risk situations than would have been the case if a sole (or even dual) backer(s) had to shoulder the entire financing risk. Syndication also combines the expertise of a number of venture capitalists behind the leader, usually to the ultimate benefit of all. The UK venture capital industry is not yet as efficient with syndication. Too many partner funds persist in duplicating the due diligence process of the syndicate leader, attempting to insert their own preferred deal structures and jockeying for aftercare priorities.

High-technology funds

There are few UK venture capital funds dedicated to investing in high- or advanced-technology industries. Most are broad-spread or general funds, investing across the spectrum of technology – including traditional manufacturing or service industries. There are no more than a handful of funds that specialise in high-technology seed capital or start-ups; most of these are captive, in-house venture capital funds of larger organisations.

A characteristic of high-technology funds is that they tend to focus on a limited number or range of technologies and industry sectors. Another common feature is that they are staffed by experienced managers with technical qualifications, supported by a formal or informal panel of scientific advisers – mostly academics or members of the relevant research institutes. These high-tech funds are almost universally hands-on participants in the management of their investee. They are also distinguished by a vigorous willingness to build their own deals through identifying areas of scientific R & D which may have commercial potential; forming companies to exploit such potential; then hiring professional managers to join the original scientific innovators if the latter choose to 'go commercial'.

For a fund to assume a high-tech style is inadvisable unless it fulfils these characteristics. If it does not have the internal and/or external resources with which to appraise proposals and nurture investments, the fund is likely to achieve a performance below commercial limits of tolerance due to an excessive failure rate. The only advisable way a general or broad-spread fund should participate in high-tech projects is as a junior and passive partner to an experienced high-tech fund or with an industrial partner as syndicate leader. Too many funds currently invest in technically advanced projects about which their understanding is inadequate; the burnt fingers are now beginning to smart, and the original blank cheques to bounce.

Focusing on chosen sectors is a difficult, indeed hazardous business.

The pace of technological change today is so rapid that borders between technologies are eroding and once-distinct industry sectors are merging. A prime example is that between data processing and telecommunications.

Only if a fund can focus effectively and sufficiently finely, however, will it be able to create its own investments – which is a crucial factor in the specialised deal flow of high-tech funds, setting them apart from the majority of venture capital funds which are broad-spread and rely, more passively, upon the general pool of venture capital deals available to most players in the market.

US experience has demonstrated that a high-tech fund must achieve a top quartile performance (in the 40–60% range) as measured by its IRR (internal rate of return) to compensate for the significantly higher risks inherent in high-tech as opposed to more general investments. As yet, no UK high-tech fund has existed long enough to demonstrate whether it is possible to match comparable, successful US funds' performance by investing in UK-based businesses.

Technology transfer

A fundamental problem with UK high-tech businesses is the relatively limited domestic market size. Exploitation of the world's largest technology market, the United States – and, indeed, defence against Japanese and US import competition in the United Kingdom – often cannot be achieved effectively without successful technology transfer. The concept of technology transfer is the licensing in or out of key technology components, particularly with US-based businesses as the licensor or licensee. One important function of a high-tech fund's management is to play an active, often leading role in the technology transfer process.

The high-tech venture capitalist frequently initiates the strategic discussion with the entrepreneur, which decides whether the business is to go it alone and attempt to exploit the international and particularly the US market through exports, local manufacture or some form of local joint venture. The optimal risk/reward ratio is often achieved by limiting the direct scope of operations to the domestic UK market, while seeking out a 'host' vehicle into which the UK technology can be licensed.

The process can be equally effective in reverse, where there is, for example, US technology to be exploited in the UK or on the Continent. The high-tech venture capitalist – using his US links – can identify a UK host vehicle, marry the two and make an investment in the UK business and possibly in its US partner as well. Advent Technology is a pioneering example of this process. The search for appropriate 'hosts', whether in the United Kingdom or the United States, is where the hands-on high-technology fund can play an active, innovative and important part in technology transfer.

An obvious but key requirement in this process is a network of effective international links, especially with the United States, at least into an intelligence network if not into a fund or group of funds – with a wide portfolio of potential licensee hosts for UK technology or licensors to UK hosts in appropriate technology sectors. Most UK funds do not have this US link, let alone any similar feeder line into/out of continental Europe or Japan – the United States' innovatory rival in the major technologies. To forge such links does not necessarily mean that the UK venture capitalist will seek to invest in the 'partner' fund in the United States, for example, or vice versa. Such cross-investment can well develop with time, but sometimes it may be essential in order to weld the bond in the first place.

The nature of such a link is essentially that of bilateral trading partners between whom at least a 'preferred nation' arrangement exists even if exclusivity cannot be granted. Each partner should thus benefit from the added value attributed to their respective investments from licensing in or out. Licensing brings fees to the licensor, and technology – hence enhanced trading prospects – to the licensee.

A number of UK funds, such as Advent, APA (Alan Patricof Associates), Venture Founders, Alta-Berkeley Associates and Baring Brothers Hambrecht and Quist, have close US links, to the extent of having been sponsored by established US venture capital groups with significant equity positions in the UK fund's management company. Here the potential for technology transfer should be assured.

From a defensive, market-intelligence-gathering stance alone, such links will be increasingly important in the world's converging technologies. The ability to minimise an investment's expansion risks while enhancing its value in a venture capital portfolio, through technology transfer, will soon become a prime weapon in the UK high-tech fund's armoury.

An unusual and potentially highly effective form of technology transfer, thus far not exploited in the United Kingdom, is to extract R & D (preferably D) projects from large companies and develop them with venture capital resources – both finance and management. Many large, even technologically based companies have R & D projects which are peripheral to their mainstream activities, have long pay-backs or are uncertain in their risks before a satisfactory return on investment can be expected.

A *technological venture partnership* (TVP) between a professional venture capital fund, the relevant large company project team(s) and their parent organisation is an attractive and efficient means of taking the risk off the parent company's balance sheet and its limited financing abilities, and the pressure off its short-term earnings record and its general management's limited time. The structure of such a TVP can allow for a number of alternative futures for the TVP and its individual component projects. They may be capable of an independent future (even a share listing), or the original parent may wish to regain 100% control, or they may be saleable to another business which can more directly exploit the project's commercial potential.

Many such projects will, of course, fail. It is possible for a TVP to allow its investors, including the original parent, to offset any unrecovered costs against their mainstream profits. TVPs are likely to become an important part of the venture capital industry over the next decade, given an unfettering of corporate wills and a favourable tax regime.

Spin-offs

Growing a successful high-technology business is singularly hazardous. Timescales are ever-compressing, the 'key people mix' frequently does not work, and there are many competitors – all more or less at the same stage of development.

The UK venture capital industry does not yet show much evidence of a frequently successful high-tech business creation – the *spin-off*. In the United States, spin-offs are a familiar occurrence, especially in the electronics technology centres of California and Massachusetts.

Spin-offs involve a team of experienced people who have left their current employer to pursue their own project(s) by establishing an independent business, often with venture capitalist backers. A spin-off carries substantially less risk than a solo (or duo) entrepreneur-based start-up, for a number of reasons:

(a) The team has probably worked together for long enough to be an effective fighting force, and any 'people fit' problems have been resolved.
(b) The project has already been developed considerably towards market exploitation before the team leaves the current employer.
(c) Any missing pieces of the technological jigsaw are likely to have

been discovered, courtesy of the current employer's R & D facilities and its spending power.

Spin-offs enjoy a much lower failure rate rather than other types of start-up. There is much more likely to be a successful outcome with a spin-off than with a university-originated high-tech company, whose team usually has no management experience. However, with a spin-off there may be ethical problems relating to who owns the rights to the products, processes (and even concepts) which the spin-off team takes with it from its current employer.

Many spin-offs themselves spawn spin-offs – the classic example being Fairchild, which sired National Semi-Conductor among others, which itself sired still other Silicon Valley firms. It has been estimated that 100 businesses have evolved through generations of spin-offs from Fairchild over the past 20 years or so. Sperry Rand, which spawned Control Data, and IBM, which spawned Amdahl, are two more spin-off ancestors.

In Europe, spin-offs are hardly noticeable as yet, apart from Silicon Glen's progeny from IBM and Burroughs. The United Kingdom's Rodime is a successful example of a Burroughs spin-off in Scotland, but there are few others. British and continental European managers are still security-conscious and 'corporation man' has dominated European business for too long.

There are signs that, with some fiscal encouragement from Government by removing the current penalties on executive share options, the United Kingdom may well be the first European country to experience spin-offs. The UK venture capital community must also be bolder in encouraging bright teams of would-be entrepreneurs to leave their current large company employers. Perhaps we all have too much cautious respect for or fear of the reaction of national majors such as GEC, Plessey, Ferranti, Philips, Siemens, Thomson and the others. In the United Kingdom the development of the TVP may be one way of moving towards the highly fruitful spin-off culture of the United States.

General-spread or non-technology funds

Often today, venture capital investment is taken to mean the creation or support of new businesses in advanced technologies. In the United States, less than a third of all venture capital goes into new businesses, with nearly half of all investments in low or medium technologies and traditional industries. Few US venture capital funds are exclusively high-tech orientated, and the same is true of the United Kingdom, where only one fund in ten has a genuine high-tech specialisation.

Most venture capital funds, in both the United States and the United Kingdom, are 'general-spread' funds. Their investments will largely be in existing proven businesses which may apply high technology to their engineering, chemical or other processes but which are fundamentally low- or medium-technology businesses. Examples include food manufacturing, metals processing, mechanical engineering, plastics conversion, construction, transport, catering and retailing.

Low-technology businesses may not have the exceptional growth trajectories and high exit multiples which can apply in high technology, but neither do they carry the extreme downside risks associated with high-tech investment. In low technology there is likely to be a more stable market, identifiable competitors and a pattern of known customers and suppliers. The rate of market change is usually broadly predictable, and product life cycles are not as frighteningly short as is increasingly the case with high tech.

All these characteristics of low-technology investments in traditional industries might appear to be less than tempting to a venture capitalist seeking a minimum rate of return in the 25–30% range. What is often forgotten, however, is that aggressive entrepreneurs who know their markets can generate new business surprisingly fast and profitably, even in low growth markets.

A successful low-technology investment can result from an entrepreneurial team, experienced in a particular sector, outperforming other companies in that sector through a combination of superior marketing and greater operating efficiency. It can also result from 'niche' positioning by a small business to dominate a small industrial sector that has a growth rate in excess of the overall industry. A further possibility is the marketing of a new product or service in the United Kingdom which, although low-technology, has not yet reached British shores, e.g. fast food restaurants. Similarly, the marketing of an existing product in a new, more effective way can bring success in low-technology investments (e.g. discount grocery stores, video film shops, tyre and exhaust centres).

The need for hands-on management in low-technology venture capital investment is not eliminated; sound industrial advice on business strategy, management structure and acquisitions can still add value to the investment. Technological uncertainties or technical inadequacies in management are likely to be less critical than in high tech but, with the all-pervasive penetration of modern technologies in most industries, lack of awareness in this area can still damage the prospects for a low-technology business.

By avoiding a concentration on high-technology and early-stage investments, a venture capital fund can spread its risks. It can achieve a greater degree of portfolio balance by investing in later-stage or development capital situations, including buy-outs. Apart from reducing the downside risk of loss in the portfolio, a general-spread fund should also benefit from an earlier realisation record through disposal of the more mature investments in its portfolio. A further feature of general funds is an ability to generate income from these later-stage investments at the outset – the more mature businesses being capable of servicing preferred equity with dividends, without damaging cash flow or seriously reducing the business's asset base.

In early-stage investments, whether high-technology or not, the financing instrument is usually total-risk ordinary equity, with little prospect of dividend income for a number of years. The backers of venture capital funds, as well as the funds' investee companies, should be clear as to whether income is expected or not, to avoid the disappointment and conflicts which will otherwise occur – and they most certainly do occur.

The concept of surrendering income today for capital gain tomorrow – or in a few years at least – is well understood by the early-stage and high-technology specialists. They are really at the sharp end of the venture capital industry, while the general-spread funds are the general practitioners, albeit often 'hands-on' in style of operation.

The evidence from US performance comparisons is not conclusive, in that early-stage and high-technology funds are matched in overall performance by the more successful general funds. The conclusion must be that a professional venture capitalist can be successful either at general practice or as a specialist. This is comforting for UK funds, the majority of which are generalists at present – including almost all the Business Expansion Scheme funds.

It is probably the case, however, that there are comparatively more below-par general than specialist funds – allowing for the fact that there are far more general funds, both in the United Kingdom and in the United States.

There are difficulties inherent in operating a general fund where early-stage or high-technology investments are concerned. The fund's mangement team is unlikely to possess the same degree of specific technical expertise as does the team of a specialist fund. Outside advisers or consultants will be relied on more fully, without having a venture capitalist to second-guess them – sometimes with unsatisfactory results.

Next, in seeking a balance between income and capital growth/gain, a general fund tends to look for income on most, if not all investments, even where an income yield is most inappropriate. This confusion of aims does not help a general fund's image in the early-stage or high-technology markets, and many general funds consequently steer away from such investments as a whole. The dilemma is, unfortunately, that a general fund which does not seed its solid later-stage/development capital portfolio with a leavening of early-stage investments is likely to perform below par, by comparison both with its competitors and with its own backers' expectations.

A successful general fund must also adopt a hybrid approach to its investment aftercare. To tackle early-stage or high-technology investments satisfactorily requires a different approach to aftercare. However, the specialist fund's hands-on skills of active participation in investee management's decision-making are not regularly found in general funds. There may be one or two team members in the general fund who specialise in certain technologies or in start-up projects. An alternative or supplementary tactic is to develop a 'stud list' of industrially experienced managers who join the investee's board and act as the prime hands-on resource, the venture capitalist partnering this guru-cum-independent director as junior partner and financial watchdog.

A successful general fund's management will resemble that of a specialist fund in that the skills mix will include industrial experience as well as financial expertise. There is likely to be a greater emphasis on venture capital techniques and information monitoring and a lesser emphasis on specific technological knowledge.

All in all, the specialist fund venture capitalist is likely to be as much at ease managing one of his investments as he is running his portfolio, while the general fund will tend to have an industrially experienced team capable of advising, supporting and assessing its investees but not inclined or even capable of managing them.

Deal flow

The successful specialist fund has a clear – and limited – internal sector or technology focus, an identifiable market image and an ability to create its own deals. In time it will be able to develop a flow of proposals which are within the chosen specialist range. The 'strike rate' will be low, in terms of investments completed from proposals made. Statistics vary from fund to fund, but a one in 50 or 80, i.e. a 1–2% ratio is probably par for the course from some 400 genuine proposals each year. The management team will carry out in-depth investigations into those it regards as serious prospects for completion, representing less than 20% of the proposals received. Each venture capitalist may complete 2–3 deals annually out of 10–15 serious investigations.

In the future, with increasing competition among venture capital funds, a specialist is more likely than a general fund to be able to carve out a continuing market niche within its own chosen activity area – whether the specialism is early-stage, technology-based or regionally based. The sustainable market position of a successful specialist fund will be due partly to its reputation for knowledge and skills within its specialism, and partly to its clarity of purpose in an overcrowed market-place.

The task for broad-spread or general funds is more difficult. They have a wider spectrum of proposals which they are prepared to handle, they are not easily differentiated from the others and, unlike specialist funds, they generally have too broad a market-place to effectively develop their own deals. A general fund will tend to be a passive receiver of referred proposals, either from financial intermediaries such as accountants, solicitors, stockbrokers and merchant bankers, or, when it is a 'captive' fund, from sister limbs of its parent organisation.

The 'strike rate' for a general fund is, paradoxically, usually higher than for a specialist fund at around 5%, or one investment made in 20 serious proposals received. This arises simply from the wider spectrum of 'possibles' that a general fund will consider, not necessarily from a coarser mesh in the general fund's screening and due diligence standards.

Aftercare in a general fund will not be intense across its entire portfolio – unlike a specialist fund – because of the significant, often dominant proportion of established and professionally managed investee businesses. A general fund's venture capitalists can thus monitor up to ten investments each, of which, it is hoped, only two or three will require the degree of active aftercare which is the norm for early-stage or high-tech investments. The hands-on aftercare in the latter investments means that each venture capitalist in a specialist fund will manage no more than five or six investments each.

A prognosis for the future deal flow of general funds is that they will have increasing problems in attracting the better proposals. Unless they are captives in organisations such as the clearing banks or merchant banks, where there is a constant flow of proposals from in-house clients of the sister limbs, they will have to develop one or more features which give them a clear and attractive market image.

Among the options for an independent general fund looking to secure its future deal flow are to:

(a) become a specialist fund, focusing on one or a limited number of technologies, on early-stage investments, buy-outs or another part of the venture capital spectrum or on a limited geographical area of the United Kingdom;

(b) market the advantages of the non-competitive and complementary nature of the independent fund to the captive funds that seek syndicate partners; it is obviously preferable for a clearing-bank- or merchant-bank-related fund to seek syndicate partners that are unlikely to compete for corporate finance business or to offer banking facilities;

(c) develop a reputation for professionalism, for a quick response to proposals and for innovative financing structures, together with an active but positively supportive aftercare role;

(d) organise the team so that a specialist facility exists within it to handle early-stage and high-technology financings, while continuing to operate the fund with a broad-spread general structure and style.

In practice, the enduring and successful general funds will probably follow a combination of these options. Others will fail to recognise the need for, or will not achieve, a distinctive approach, and will struggle for an existence with little prospect of raising further finance from their disappointed backers.

Venture capital funds taxation

The Government has recognised the need to foster small companies in the United Kingdom, particularly those in various areas of technology. The imaginative Business Start-up Scheme, now the Business Expansion Scheme, shows the Government's commitment in this field.

The Government's measures have been structured to encourage the individual to invest in 'venture capital'. It is at least equally important to encourage the institutional investors along this road. Their historical reluctance to invest in long-term, unquoted, non-income-yielding opportunities is well known. But their attitude is slowly changing as they see the great industrial and technological changes now taking place, often in small, unquoted companies. They are encouraged by the returns made in the United States on venture capital investments and by the establishment in Britain of a number of specialist US-style venture capital houses that offer hands-on management as well as capital to emerging enterprises.

A simple tax anomaly is currently making it difficult for tax-paying institutional investors to finance emerging companies through the specialist venture capital funds. They pay tax on any realised capital gains twice, once when the fund sells its investment, and again when the institution sells its shares in the fund. This is clearly inequitable; it does not apply if a tax-paying institution entrusts its assets to a specialist manager to invest in quoted stocks through an investment trust, because the latter is exempt from capital gains tax. Why should a venture capital fund pay double tax on unquoted investments while a listed investments trust does not, on the very same investments – where, as is common, an investment trust joins in an unlisted company syndicate, alongside venture capitalists?

One further anomaly exists. If a venture capital fund obtains a Stock Exchange listing, using the recently revised rules for investment trusts and listed investment companies, it will again be exempted from capital gains tax. However, the purpose of a venture capital fund is long-term investment, while a Stock Exchange listing, perforce, encourages short-term performance, particularly from newly listed companies – making them vulnerable to bargain-hunting or asset-stripping predators at a stage when their realised early failures will have reduced their net asset values and before their big winners have come to fruition.

If listed investment companies or investment trusts comply in any accounting period with Section 359 of the Income and Corporation Taxes Act 1970, they will be granted exemption from capital gains tax for that period. As capital growth is the main objective of most investment companies and trusts, this represents a major advantage and avoids double taxation, i.e. of both the company and the shareholder.

To qualify for Section 359 approval, any company resident in the United Kingdom that is not a close company, and whose income is derived wholly or mainly from shares or securities, can apply for approval as an investment trust for tax purposes with respect to any accounting period provided the following main conditions are satisfied:

(a) The shares making up the company's ordinary share capital must be quoted on a recognised stock exchange in the United Kingdom.
(b) The distribution, as dividends, of surpluses arising from the

realisation of investments must be prohibited by the company's Memorandum and Articles of Association.

(c) The company must not retain in respect of any accounting period more than 15% of the income it derives from shares and securities.

(d) No holding in a company, other than in another investment trust, can represent more than 15% by value of the investing company's investments.

The difference between an investment company and an investment trust is that the former has no restriction on the percentage of its assets which may be invested in unlisted securities, while not more than 25% of the assets of an investment trust may be invested in the aggregate of unlisted securities, the remainder normally being composed of listed securities.

Investment companies do, however, have to pay corporation tax on their income net of management expenses. Since the investment objective is capital growth rather than income growth, this requirement is not too onerous. Furthermore, many unlisted companies in which they invest will be at an early stage of their development and are likely to earn a higher return by reinvesting their cash flow in the business rather than by distributing it through high dividends to shareholders. It appears that the legislative framework governing investment companies is exactly what is needed to further mobilise UK institutional funds towards venture capital investment.

Specifically, an amendment to Section 359 of the Income and Corporation Taxes Act 1970 would permit incorporation of venture capital funds, which could then raise funds from any corporate investor under the investment company legislation but *without the requirement to be listed*. The venture capital funds would then be exempt from capital gains tax on any funds realised, but each investing institution would be liable to capital gains tax on its investment in the fund, subject to its own tax status. Thus an institutional investor would enjoy the same tax regime as it would have enjoyed had it made a direct investment.

14 The role of the State

It may seem anomalous that, in the white heat of private-sector competition which is the environment of today's small businesses, the State has any role to play other than a fiscal one of reducing taxation. In fact, despite the avowedly independent and capitalist world of venture capital, the UK Government has made a significant contribution to the resurgence of the smaller-business sector and its supporting cast in the venture capital community.

There are five main aspects of the State's recent role in the United Kingdom's venture capital boom:

(a) Fiscal and direct grant financing programmes for the small companies themselves.
(b) Specific State-subsidised incentive schemes to channel private-sector finance into smaller businesses.
(c) The State's own venture capital institutions.
(d) Privatisation of State-owned activities and partnership with private-sector venture capital.
(e) General encouragement of the entrepreneur and his backers through specialist advice, public exhortation and rewards given through the Honours system, and political pressure on the Civil Service to favour the small-business sector.

Fiscal and other incentives

A recent Minister for Small Business, the post itself an innovation in 1979, stated in 1983 that over 200 new measures had been introduced during those four years, specifically favouring the small-business sector in general and the advanced technology areas in particular.

It is not intended here to provide an exhaustive survey of State assistance for small business, whether from central or local Government. Many excellent and thorough guides already exist and are updated regularly. Each budget brings some new schemes and amendments to current schemes, so that the whole area is in constant motion. Perhaps the best guides to Government grants are produced by the leading firms of accountants. One of them, Peat Marwick Mitchell, even has a weekly updating service, by local authority area, available on Prestel.

In summary, the broad areas of *central Government* asistance and incentives to the small-business sector are noted below. Many of them, apart from taxation, also apply to larger businesses.

Taxation. Reduced rates of corporation tax below £500,000 profits; business relief on capital transfer tax; tax relief on loan interest for share purchase; start-up relief against previous employment income; retirement relief.

Regional assistance. Assisted areas (special development; development and intermediate areas) – regional development grants; selective financial assistance; EEC low-interest loans; government factories and government contract preferences.

Other measures apply to rural areas, new towns, inner urban areas, steel redundancy areas, enterprise zones, science parks and European regional development areas.

Technology programmes. Micro-electronics application project; computer skills training; industrial robots support; flexible manufacturing assistance; software development; fibre optics and opto-electronics; telecommunications projects.

Product and process development. Small engineering firms investment scheme; selective assistance for manufacturing investment; support for innovation (product development grants).

Other. Training schemes for small businesses; export marketing support; public purchasing.

Local governments have also developed active programmes of support for small businesses within their areas. These programmes vary, but include grants, loans, rent-free council-owned factories, rate-free periods and even equity finance. A number of local authorities have developed their own enterprise boards or equivalent, including Greater London, West Yorkshire, West Midlands, Merseyside, Nottingham and Greater Manchester – although the fate of these following the abolition of the Metropolitan counties is uncertain. There are more than 50 local enterprise agencies, supported in part by the relevant local authority, and a number of small business centres, economic development units, enterprise workshops, small industry groups, etc. Most of these organisations provide additional rather than alternative finance to that available from the central Government.

In the autumn of 1984, the system of regional development grants and selective financial incentives was changed, but there are provisions for a transitional period. Changes to the existing system include new boundaries to the assisted areas; a switch in emphasis from capital-intensive to jobs-intensive projects; regional development grants based on new investment projects rather than on *ad hoc* capital expenditure; certain service industries to benefit specifically; modernisation projects which do not qualify for regional development grants may still qualify for selective financial assistance; and small firms to be exempted from new capital expenditure per job limits.

Incentives for private-sector investment

There are two distinct aspects of the State's encouragement to the private sector to invest in small business – the Loan Guarantee Scheme and the Business Expansion Scheme, referred to in Chapter 2. Both of these schemes are non-directional, supporting all kinds of young business enterprise rather than concentrating on the newer industries and technologies.

Loan Guarantee Scheme (LGS)

First introduced in 1980, with an initial allocation of £600 million, the LGS is a Government-subsidised medium-term loan scheme for small businesses. Loans are made by some 30 lending institutions, including clearing banks, merchant banks, ICFC and others. These loans are 70% underwritten by the Government; thus the lender is at risk of only 30% of the amount lent. There are several non-qualifying types of enterprise, including property, travel agencies, agriculture, betting and gambling, financial services, night-clubs and a number of others.

The maximum amount per borrower is £75,000, repayable over 2–7 years, and the 'insurance' premium charged by the Government to the lenders, which is invariably passed on to the borrower, is 5%. LGS loans are thus not cheap, as the lender will also charge its normal small business rate, bringing the interest to about 5–7% per annum above base rate, a total currently of 19–20% per annum. A particular advantage of LGS loans was that personal guarantees by the borrower were not required. Recently, however, the rules have changed and personal security is now sought.

At present about £500 million has been drawn down under the LGS, going to some 15,000 businesses – evidence certainly of a real demand. Whether the majority of businesses receiving LGS loans would have received loans of some sort in its absence is unproved, but it is likely that the LGS has to some extent filled the small-ticket equity gap discussed in Chapter 12.

The LGS has been criticised for providing bankers with guarantees of the highest possible quality for loans which would have been made in any case, and for giving bankers the opportunity to shift to the tax-payers their risk on some of their smaller, doubtful debts. The Government, sensitive to these suggestions, asked independent accoun-tants to carry out an interim investigation into the results of the scheme. While admitting that there might be some justification in these criti-cisms, their report also highlighted a greater than expected failure rate in companies receiving LGS loans – over 20% of all LGS recipients – with forecasts of eventual failures ranging as high as one in three.

This experience tends to confirm the view that the LGS is performing an equity role in businesses too small to attract professional venture capital, bridging the funding gap until such companies grow large enough to justify an investment of at least £100,000 – which is where the range of professional venture capital investment begins. Most venture capitalists, while agreeing that these small businesses really require equity rather than debt at the stage when they seek LGS loans, will admit that the LGS does provide a useful function in protecting them from the higher costs and relative unattractiveness of small-ticket equity investment.

Business Expansion Scheme (BES)

The BES has already been referred to a number of times. The successor of the Business Start-up Scheme (BSS), the BES was introduced in the Finance Act 1983 and became operative in August 1983; since then more than 30 specialist BES fund management groups have been established, raising a total of nearly £100 million through more than 50 separate funds for equity investment in growing businesses.

The BES is for private investors, not banks or institutions, to invest new capital in qualifying smaller companies. The individual obtains tax relief at his marginal rate of income tax, up to a total of £40,000 per annum (£80,000 for couples). Higher amounts can be invested under the Venture Capital Scheme, but here tax offset against income is available only on loss of the investment.

The BES tax relief is available whether or not the investment is lost, but only when the investment is made. Thus the many fund management groups which have gathered individuals' contributions under their 'umbrella' must be fully invested within the particular tax year those contributions were made, in order for their subscribers to obtain tax relief.

Apart from the new shares rule, there are other constraints on BES investments. Not all trades qualify, as with the LGS; people investing in their own businesses cannot get the tax relief; the shares must be held for five years and the investee company cannot be listed for three years if a claw-back of the tax relief is to be avoided; no individual can control more than 30% of his investee company. Although USM companies do not qualify, those traded on OTC markets do.

It is uncertain how much BES investment is being made directly rather than through the approved funds mentioned above, but the amounts of tax relief expected by the Inland Revenue would suggest an annual investment rate of £100 million over the next three years. If achieved, that would add 50% to the amount currently invested in venture capital by the 70 or so non-BES funds active in the UK industry. Unless demand by small businesses grows similarly over that period, which is possible, the BES funds will have to eat into their non-BES competitors' market share or find niches not filled by their competitors, or both.

Recognition of the competitive threat to their existing venture capital activities, together with the opportunities afforded by the BES, has encouraged a number of venture capital funds to set up a parallel BES fund. Among such dual vehicles are those of Charterhouse, County Bank, Baronsmead, Lazards, Granville & Co. and Electra Investment Trust.

The majority of BES funds, however, are managed independently of other venture capital funds. There is some doubt in the venture capital industry as to whether all these BES funds have the kind of experienced, professional management required for active portfolio aftercare, as well as the essential investigative skills. Some BES funds have recognised this potential problem, and are looking to co-invest with established venture capital funds – the latter leading in the investigatory and aftercare roles.

There are undoubtedly opportunities for BES and institutional venture capital funds to invest together through a limited syndication:

(a) Where the entrepreneur does not want a single dominant investor, whether the BES fund or the institutional fund. This co-operation is particularly appropriate where some replacement capital ('money out') is involved as well as new money for expansion or de-gearing, since the BES fund cannot buy existing shares.
(b) Where there is a requirement for more than ordinary equity, be it convertible loan stock, preference shares or preferred ordinary shares, since the BES fund cannot invest in securities bearing a predetermined coupon or rate of interest; hence the advantage of joining forces with a non-BES fund, which can do all of these things.
(c) Where the BES funds become fully invested within the tax year, do not raise further monies but still have a deal flow from sources they wish to satisfy; bearing in mind their next year's fund, they will seek a friendly referral.
(d) Where a BES fund has a proposition that exceeds its own limits for any single investment, usually 20% of the total fund, in which case it will seek to syndicate the investment.
(e) Where a BES fund is unable to follow its money in an existing investment requiring a further round of financing, because it is fully invested and has not been able to raise another fund.

In the last two categories, it is theoretically possible for one BES fund to ask another BES fund to join in, but the practical reality is that each BES fund has its own rules as to fees charged to the investee company, and also option arrangements which differ greatly from fund to fund. In many cases it will be easier to syndicate with a non-BES fund.

The performance of BES funds cannot be judged after only a few months' investment, but their general trend away from the early-stage businesses favoured by the Business Start-up Scheme is likely to ensure a lower failure rate than that experienced by the BSS funds. Whether this is what was intended when the Government loosened the restrictions on the BSS in the 1983 Budget is unclear. What is undeniable, however, is that BES investment is shy of the young, start-up company which the BSS was originally designed to encourage.

There are currently some serious contraints on the achievement of the BES' architects' intentions. There are four broad aspects, as outlined below.

Time window. Under the present rules the BES investor receives his tax relief only from the date of investment in a business. When he invests through an approved fund – which is the case with the vast majority of BES investors – if the fund is not itself fully invested at the end of the tax year, he loses part of his relief for that year. Not only is he somewhat disappointed to find that he has sheltered less of his income than he expected when subscribing to the fund, but also he is probably resentful that the fund (in most cases) has itself enjoyed the benefits of interest on the uninvested portion of his subscription monies.

Awareness of this investor sensitivity by the professional BES fund managers has the possibly risky consequence that they will scurry around trying to invest the remaining liquid balances before the year-end – not necessarily always in the sort of proposition they would choose, were it not for the artificiality of the curtain closing over their time window. Performance will naturally suffer, and perhaps make it more difficult for the fund to raise money at some future date. To return the uninvested monies at the year-end is not an entirely satisfactory answer unless the return includes the interest which the investor will have forgone in making his original subscription.

Overseas activities. At present businesses receiving BES finance are barred from expanding their companies into overseas sales or manufacturing operations. If a BES recipient breaches certain complex guidelines, his investors lose part of their tax relief. Many entrepreneurs, faced with this potential clamp on their business strategy, turn away from BES funding.

Share quotation. While a BES investor has no difficulty investing directly in a company quoted on the OTC markets, if a company in which he has previously invested gains a USM or full listing within three years he loses part of his relief. Again, an entrepreneur may well hesitate to take BES funding if he is going to be faced with hassle from his investors should he choose to go to the share markets within three years.

Young business. The BES arose largely because its predecessor, the BSS, failed to raise significant amounts – some £15 million in two years against expectations of £100 million annually. The BES rules were extended to include mature businesses as well as the start-ups and young businesses (less than five years old) of the BSS.

The results of the BES are that more than £75 million of funds have been raised since mid-1983, in the investors' expectations that these monies will be put into safe, established companies. All the evidence from the activities of the approved BES funds is that this is happening.

Where does that leave the early-stage entrepreneur, for whom the whole exercise was originally designed? He is most likely as bereft of equity funding as he was before the BSS and BES were conceived.

The encouragement to BES sponsors to invest in solid, unexciting, established and probably non-growth businesses is illustrated in the example below:

An illustration of the effect of tax relief obtained under the Business Expansion Scheme

The result of an investment over five years would be:		
Marginal tax rate	60%	50%
Actual net cost of £10,000 gross investment	4,000	5,000
Investment proceeds after capital gains tax (assumes investment sold for £15,000, i.e. only 8.5% compound growth)	14,130	14,130
Total increase over five years	253%	182%
This represents an annual compound after tax return on net investment of:	28%	23%

State venture capital institutions

In Chapter 2 the original activities of the BTG (British Technology Group) and the SDA, WDA and NIDA (Scottish, Welsh and Northern Ireland Development Agencies, respectively) were discussed. While the regional agencies remain in possession of their wide powers to encourage small and growing businesses in their territories, the BTG's wings have been severely clipped. Not only has the NEB role of the BTG been terminated, so that the BTG can no longer take an active role in equity investments on its own account, but the NRDC activity of high-technology promotion and technology transfer has been deprived of its exclusive right to the research and development output of Government research establishments and the universities.

Whether these agencies, first-tier (BTG, SDA, WDA, NIDA) or second-tier, will endure is not certain. The metamorphosis of the NEB/NRDC is an example of how a combination of changed political philosophy and a burgeoning private-sector venture capital activity can reduce the State's role. At present, however, particularly in the regions, small business entrepreneurs will often find their early-stage funding at least partly from these Government-financed bodies.

In general, the State's own industrial financing arms are staffed by a mixture of 'insiders' – secondees from the Civil Service or local government – and 'outsiders' from industry or private-sector financial institutions. In recent years, there has been a distinct trend towards the latter source, including a sprinkling of seasoned venture capitalists from private-sector funds. Indeed, the BTG, SDA and WDA have gone so far as to establish separate venture capital arms with their own specialist skills in the field.

The BTG has also disposed of a group of its own 'nursery' investments to the private sector, while retaining a residual shareholding. This venture is Grosvenor Development Capital, an early-stage advanced-technology fund, whose partners are Equity Capital for Industry, British Rail Pension Fund, County Bank and the BTG.

It is inevitable, however, that the investment motivation of the State agencies is not always primarily one of commercial return, and thus it is unusual for an entrepreneur to find venture capital expertise in these agencies equivalent to that available in the private sector – although the State bodies' financing terms and conditions may often be more attractive than those of the private-sector funds.

While there has been speculation about a Northern Region Development Agency and a West Midlands equivalent, the current mood and policies of the Government give every indication of encouraging the private sector to fulfil the United Kingdom's capital expectations – with the exception of the regional agencies' limited role. What is being actively pursued, however, is the partnership of private-sector and Government establishments in the privatisation of State businesses and the development of new businesses from State-originated technology.

Privatisation and private-sector partnership

Since 1980 a number of major State-owned industrial establishments have been sold into the private sector through stock market listings. These include Amersham International, the National Freight Corporation, Enterprise Oil, part of British Transport Hotels and, imminently, the Royal Ordnance Factories, Sealink and British Rail Engineering. These *privatisations* have not yet fallen into the ambit of the UK venture capital industry, but several investments in the NEB's portfolio have been hived down, in partnership with venture capitalists.

Logica, the United Kingdom's leading independent software house, is a shining example of an NEB privatisation which has since achieved a full stock market listing. Celltech, which was initiated by the NEB, has received second-round finance entirely from private-sector investment institutions, including venture capital funds.

Further NEB privatisations are BUE (British Underwater Engineering), Monotype – the hive-down in this case being led by Grosvenor itself – Inmos, Logica, CAP and Pearce Technology.

A second and perhaps more important aspect of present Government policy is the partnering of public-sector research and development bodies by the venture capital community. In the past the State-owned

National Research and Development Corporation had a virtual monopoly over this technology transfer role. Soon after the NRDC's incorporation into the British Technology Group, the NRDC's exclusivity was terminated. Since then, the venture capital industry has been busy constructing bridgeheads into many of these establishments. In certain cases, formal or informal clubs have been set up to exploit a particular establishment's specialisation. The Agricultural Genetics Company is a specialist fund set up by a group of venture capitalists to exploit the technology of the Agricultural Research Council. A formal club of venture capitalists has grouped around the Ministry of Defence's prime R & D establishments, under the name Defence Technology Enterprises.

These initiatives have a common aim: to take the research potential of a scientific establishment and from it develop commercial applications. The next stage of actually launching products or processes based on successful applications development is likely to be reached by one (or both) of two routes – licensing out to host companies, in which the venture capital partners of the 'application club' may well themselves invest, or the setting up by the venture capitalists of new companies to exploit the developed technology. The latter course involves perhaps the most creative aspect of hands-on venture capital management – the ability to structure a business from scratch and, above all, to attract key managers to build the business.

Undoubtedly, there will be more such collaboration between venture capitalists and Government scientists, which should, in time, bring substantial benefits to the small-business sector in addition to reducing the cost to the Exchequer of central research establishment budgets.

Government R & D spending totals over £3.5 billion, with Defence accounting for half of this substantial amount and Education/Science for one quarter. No other sector accounts for as much as 10%, with Industry taking only 8% and Energy 6%. There must be significant potential for civil or commercial exploitation of this substantial R & D effort which has, after all, been funded by the taxpayer. In the United States, much computer-related products growth has arisen from the stimulus of NASA, the space programme, and the Pentagon's defence R & D programme.

General support

Apart from the specific measures to aid small businesses in general and venture capital in particular, referred to in this chapter, the Government has given special emphasis to the encouragement of the entrepreneur.

The Department of Trade and Industry's Small Firms Service, with its 15 centres throughout the country, has developed a specialist role in the past few years, both in publicising the activities of the many varieties of local enterprise agency in its localities and in providing free consultancy advice for the smaller business.

The Honours system has, for the first time in half a century, given exposure to the small business entrepreneur. A number of successful small business leaders have already been honoured, and others will follow. Whatever the public's view of the Honours system, the exposure given to the entrepreneur has, at the very least, drawn attention to the small-business sector.

In the early 1980s, the Queen's Awards for Exports and Technology benefited the smaller business significantly – another example of the Government's wish to encourage this sector. The Government's purchasing policies are currently being examined to see how the United Kingdom's companies might be given greater opportunities to supply the public sector.

Further back in the entrepreneurial pipeline, in 1984 the Department of Education and Science carried out some fundamental rethinking about the ways in which technological and business subjects are taught in schools. This initiative, albeit long-term in its benefits, is yet another important step in the move to develop a new entrepreneurial Britain in the area of the advanced technologies.

For those who have been active in UK venture capital for a decade or more, never before has there been a feeling of official favour and encouragement as at present.

15 Continental Europe

Birth of European venture capital

Before 1980, it was probably the case that the UK venture capital industry was a quarter century behind that of the United States. Since 1980, the United Kingdom has reduced the time-lag to about a decade. On the other hand, the United Kingdom leads other European countries, but by only five years or so. Since 1982, there has been a surge of venture capital development in continental Europe, particularly in France, the Netherlands, Sweden and Belgium.

European Venture Capital Association

In August 1983, a European Venture Capital Association (EVCA) was formed from 40 funds, of which 11 are British in origin. France has ten members, the Netherlands six, Belgium four, Ireland three and West Germany three. There are two members from Italy and one from Denmark. A list of EVCA members will be found in Appendix B.

One of the principal objectives of the EVCA is to examine and discuss the management of and investment in venture capital in the European Community, with a view to promoting further development of the industry across national borders. Other objectives are: to encourage the provision of equity finance for innovation and for small-to-medium-sized businesses; to establish and maintain the highest standards of business conduct and professional competence among its members; to foster the promotion, research and analysis of venture capital activity in Europe and facilitate contact with policy-makers, research institutions, universities, trade associations and other relevant bodies; and to further promote the use of equity markets as appropriate to the exit needs of venture capital investors and investees.

Full membership of the EVCA is open only to those companies and individuals able to demonstrate substantial activity in the management of equity or quasi-equity financing for the start-up or development of small companies with significant growth potential. Members are also expected to have as their main objective the pursuit of long-term capital gains and must be able to provide active management support to their investees. In addition, they must have their main centre of activities and principal investments within the European Community.

EEC Commission activities

The EEC Commission, whose Directorate General XIII was largely responsible for the original initiative to launch the EVCA, has had a four-year programme to enhance the establishment and growth of what are known as New Technology Based Firms (NTBFs). This programme was set up with substantial funding from the EEC Budget. A further initiative of the EEC Commission was the European Year of Small and Medium-Sized Enterprises (SMEs) in 1983. SMEs are unquoted businesses employing fewer than 500 people. NTBFs are not as easily defined – no widely accepted definition exists to date.

The objective of these programmes to favour the small business entrepreneur is twofold: the harmonisation of legal and fiscal practice throughout the European Community, and the provision of special financial assistance to the EEC's NTBFs and SMEs. Whatever can be done along these lines, however, the fundamental problem is that of limited market potential for these NTBFs and SMEs, particularly the barriers to trade within the EEC that prevent Europe from becoming a market comparable in size to that of North America.

There is much to be done in this area, partly through the destruction of nationally erected administrative and other barriers to trade, and partly through the deliberate exercise of preference by public purchasers for EEC goods and services, whatever their source. Until buyers' habits and choices throughout the EEC are considerably more standardised, it is unlikely, regrettably, that a genuine open market can develop.

Among the special financial instruments that the European Community offers the small-business sector are the New Community Instrument (NCI) loans, or the 'Ortoli Facility', launched in 1977. NCI loans are provided by the European Investment Bank (EIB) through agencies in each country, such as ICFC and Midland Bank in the United Kingdom. A total of about £1.3 billion has been drawn under the NCI, of which Britain has had some £70 million. Other loans are available from the EIB and the ECSC (European Coal and Steel Community), particularly in the assisted areas and areas of steel and coal closures, respectively. Interest subsidies are also available for EIB loans in certain member countries.

Apart from the activities of the EEC Commission in European venture capital, many European governments have been implementing policies to assist their small-business sectors. A brief summary of the current venture capital situation across the EEC follows, with acknowledgement of the respective contributions by leading venture capital funds in continental Europe as follows:

France – Soginnove SA (Jacques Stouff)
West Germany – Deutsche Wagnisfinanzierungsgesellschaft mbH (Karl-Heinz Fanselow)
The Netherlands – Parcom Beheer BV (Aris Wateler)
Belgium – Prominvest NV (Marc van der Stichele)
Denmark – Privatbankens Initiativfond (Bent Kiemer)
Ireland – Venture Economics (Sue Lloyd)

Country summaries

France

This is a fast-developing situation, with some ten genuine venture capital funds now in existence – mostly bank-owned or bank-backed. Three of these funds are long-standing, with a decade or more of experience behind them. There are about 40 other separate sources of small company risk capital.

European Enterprises Development (EED), set up in 1964, started the venture capital industry in France. In July 1972, a law giving fiscal incentives to shareholders enabled the first Sociétés Financières d'Innovation (SFI) to be set up. The same year, a state-owned banking institution, the Crédit National, founded Sofinnova and the bank Société Générale founded Soginnove. These two SFIs are still the leaders but there are seven others, some specialised by activity: Batinnova, Epicea, Agrinova, Idianova, Finovelec, Finovectron and Innovest – the last set up for Alsace. The total amount of the French SFIs' capital is £30 million. SFIs invest in innovating companies with a turnover up to £40 million, and their investments are in equity or convertible loans only.

Venture capital is also available from the regionally focused Sociétés de Développement Régional (SDRs) and Instituts de Participation, which supply equity to companies with a higher turnover (or to non-innovating firms) and also provide medium- and long-term loans. There are now some 18 SDRs. The first Institut de Participation and still the largest, IDI, was set up in 1970. In 1984 it increased its capital base to FFr1 billion (£90 million) through an injection of new equity from EDF (Electricité de France – the State utility). The others are regional – Siparex, IPO, Participex, IAD, IRDI, Auxitex.

In 1979 the re-formation of the Agence Nationale de Valorisation de la Recherche stimulated innovation and multiplied the venture capital opportunities. The recent Fonds Industriel de Modernisation reinforced them. The Fonds Commun de Placement à Risques (FCPR) were set up in 1983 with a maximum amount of 100 million French francs (£8 million), and should invest a minimum of 40% in shares or convertible loans of unlisted companies. By December 1983, 13 FCPRs were authorised.

Apart from general financial incentives for the small-business sector, the *prêts participatifs* are subordinated loans which can be rewarded by a mixture of interest and profits participation. These loans are made by government, a variety of public institutions, banks, insurance companies and private-sector commercial companies. Inodev (Institut pour le développement de l'innovation) initiated *prêts participatifs*, followed by CEPME and then the banks. Further incentives for venture capital investments are in the pipeline.

In January 1983 the Paris second-tier market opened. An application for a quotation is now possible for companies placing only 10% of their shares, with a simplified procedure of accounts certification and information. There are 60 stocks quoted and more are expected in the near future.

Foreign investors seem to be more and more interested in the French market. Charterhouse, which has operated in France in development capital since 1972, set up a venture capital company, Cree, in January 1984. Investors in Industry (3i) established a subsidiary in Paris in the same month. Among Siparex shareholders are Dresdner Bank, Union de Banques Suisses, 3i, the State of Kuwait and Credit Anstalt Bank Verein. Citicorp also set up a venture fund in Paris in late 1984, and Alan Patricof Associates launched a FFr100 million (£8 million) French fund during 1984.

In 1984, an initiative was taken for the first time to encourage management buy-outs in France. The Government is changing company law to favour buy-outs, and major financial groups have formed a number of joint ventures to promote them. Compagnie Financière de

Suez has joined IDI in forming the largest French venture capital fund to date (the Suez fund will also back start-ups and expansion financings), with an initial FFr200 million (£16m) capital. Paribas/Crédit du Nord Compagnie Bull/Rhône-Poulenc have set up Codific with an initial FFr40 million (£3m).

Charterhouse has joined Crédit National, Banque Industrielle et Mobilière Prince and Banque Indosuez in setting up a FFr50 million (£4.5m) fund to promote leveraged management buy-outs on the US model – under the name 'Initiative et Finance'. Crédit National has also joined with Sofinnova and Union des Assurances de Paris in starting 'Team' (Transmition d'Entreprises au Management), a FFr40 million (£3.5m) management buy-out fund.

West Germany

In the Federal Republic of Germany, loan financing has been the traditional way of boosting company resources, and the country's 'universal' banks have for many years held a pivotal role in the economy both through the provision of loans and through their quasi-monopolistic position in bringing companies onto the stock market.

Private family-owned companies play a significant role in the economic structure of the country. Almost three-quarters of all registered companies are family-owned. Of the 450 joint-stock companies on the stock exchange, some 200 are still under family influence. With smaller companies, this is the predominant situation.

There is an instinctive aversion among family companies to go public to raise equity capital. They often harbour fears about changing the intimate nature of the company and reservations about publicising their profits and stimulating their competitors.

Generally, the significance of equity as a financial instrument has been small. Looking to the banks for a loan or trying to find a wealthy partner have been the usual ways of obtaining substantial funding. But things are slowly changing, and the recession-induced slow-down in loans from the banks has sent many companies out on a search for equity capital; 1983 and 1984 saw considerable activity both in the number of companies going public and in the number of venture capital companies launched.

Though excellent profits exist for venture capital in West Germany, there are still a number of negative institutional and fiscal factors affecting equity financing. The Government is, however, actively considering certain reforms to improve the venture capital environment.

The country's oldest venture capital company, WFG, was set up in

1975 by 29 of the leading banking and credit institutions to offer equity capital to small and medium-sized companies with promising innovative potential. It now has investments of over £15 million in 42 companies. A number of other banking institutions have set up or are participating in new funds, and a lot of momentum has also been generated by large industrial concerns that have been establishing their own 'windows on technology' through venture capital.

Although capital is available, it can be fairly said that it has not been invested primarily in technical innovations. It has tended more to flow onto the so-called 'grey' capital market – into investments affording tax relief and into commodities futures. The reason is quite simple: the return on equity capital in companies in West Germany has fallen in recent years.

The reliance on bank finance can be seen from the ratio of equity capital to total assets, which is now down to around a 20% average (debt: equity gearing is 5 to 1). It is therefore understandable that the poor return from companies in the past decade has subdued the willingness of West German investors to commit themselves in this sector. It is also not surprising that two-thirds of the country's small and medium-sized companies cite financing as one of the main brakes on innovation.

In general, the tax situation favours the private investor but is less favourable for the institutional investor.

The Federal Republic has significant technical potential and also knows how to market its products and services, as can be seen from the success of its export industry.

With the introduction of innovations on their markets practically a matter of life and death for many companies, equity capital has assumed vital importance. If an innovation should turn out to be a flop, only equity capital can absorb the repercussions and can give the company the necessary staying power – particularly if this equity capital is invested by venture capitalists able to provide 'hands-on' management assistance and advice.

Of the large number of new businesses that have been set up, roughly three-quarters are in the services sector; over half of them don't last more than three years. West Germany is faced with a shortage of young entrepreneurs with a technical background. It is still rare for an experienced manager with good salary, good career prospects and adequate social security to start up on his own. For one thing, he would be regarded as somewhat peculiar by his peers. In addition, there aren't many in West Germany willing to give up the security of a permanent job. On top of that, considerable bureaucratic obstacles and social legislation, which in some cases have the effect of discouraging job creation, do not make it easy to build up a company.

However, there are now a number of experienced managers who have launched out on their own in buy-outs or in spin-off companies. There are also growing numbers of entrepreneurs who take advantage of venture capital to prepare their company for conversion into a joint-stock company (*Aktiengesellschaft*) as a means of obtaining equity capital. It is widely felt, however, that greater incentives must be created to encourage more people in West Germany to become entrepreneurs.

High-technology projects

The Federal Republic is at present unfortunately short of small-scale enterprises specialised in advanced technology. The domestic market is too small for high-technology companies to become really successful. Even the European market is not wide enough in most areas. To be successful, a company of this kind must export to the United States right from the start. And that is likely to be a great hurdle for many.

A number of venture capital companies have been formed since 1982. West Berlin is one of the fast-growing high-technology centres, where in the 18 months up to end-1984, six venture capital companies were formed mobilising some DM100 million. So great has been the influx of private capital that an innovation fund sponsored by the Berlin Senate is increasingly being regarded as superfluous. In many ways, West Berlin is seen as a test market for venture capital. The climate is also very favourable with bodies such as the Technical University and College encouraging their brightest graduates to branch out on their own in the best entrepreneurial fashion.

A major new initiative has been taken by Siemens, the Matuschka Group and TA Associates (The US Advent Venture Capital Group) in forming Techno Venture Management (TVM). TVM has a DM130 million (£35m) pool subscribed 25% by Siemens, with Daimler Benz, Mannesman, Bayer and a number of other industrial majors joining the funding group. TVM is primarily interested in advanced-technology projects.

Capital structures

Because of the tight stock exchange listing requirements and the restrictive policy of the banks that would be floating the issue, most firms are today organised as a limited liability GmbH.

It is very common for a venture capital company to take up a holding in the form of an undisclosed partnership. The contribution by the undisclosed partner goes into the assets of the partnership or limited company.

The holding does not involve any obligations to manage or work for the firm. The undisclosed contribution ranks after all other creditors in the event of insolvency, which means that it has something of the nature of equity capital. How the contribution to capital is repaid is agreed by the parties concerned. Often it will include an option to be converted into stock should the company go public. This approach enables the venture capital company to get a return without the problem of the subjective valuation of a non-quoted company. The advantage of this for the company is that there are few legal reporting requirements, a high degree of freedom and lower costs.

Going public

Financing a joint-stock corporation (AG) is, of course, by far the most interesting possibility. The institutional set-up does meet the requirements for going public. West Germany has 3.5 million private investors, the third largest figure in the West. It also has 600 investment funds that can invest in shares. Eleven companies went public in 1983 and more than 20 did so in 1984.

The country has eight stock exchanges and the equivalent of an unlisted securities market (*geregelter Freiverkehr*). It has a third institution termed *Telefonverkehr* (unregulated unofficial security dealings), which is comparable to the OTC (over-the-counter) markets in the United States and the United Kingdom, where business is conducted over the telephone.

The Netherlands

This is one of the fastest-developing venture capital markets in the EEC, with some 25 private venture capital funds and 20 other small business risk finance funds now established, and much Government encouragement for the industry. Most of the funds are bank-owned or bank-related, but several are institutionally backed.

A special measure introduced by the Government in 1981 to help provide risk capital for the small-business sector is the PPM scheme or *particulerie participatie maatschappijen*. PPMs are small-company investment funds where up to half the risk is indemnified by the Government. PPMs can invest up to 40% of their total investments outside the rather complex rules of the scheme. At present, 25 PPMs have been established, mostly launched by banks, insurance companies, pension funds and a few industrial companies. In effect, the PPMs performance is subsidised to the extent that its overall capital gains will be improved by half its losses being eliminated, due to the Government indemnification. By the end of December 1983, PPMs had invested DFl 36 million (£10 million) in some 50 businesses, of which half were existing companies and half start-ups or spin-offs.

In order to cover the whole range of ventures, small and large, the Ministry of Economic Affairs – on the advice of the Commissie Wagner, an industrial and economic policy think-tank – has established a specialised industrial project development organisation, the Maatschappij voor Industriele Projecten. This organisation principally caters for risky, large to very large projects with a minimum capital contribution of DFl 4 million (for less than 50% of the equity). Funds are provided by the Government, the National Investment Bank and a whole range of other financial institutions.

The long-established National Investment Bank supports a large number of companies with a whole gamut of secured and unsecured financial instruments (including equity capital). The bank is also associated with a few venture funds in the Netherlands through substantial equity stakes and board representation. In addition, it maintains a close liaison with all regional development companies and acts on behalf and on account of the Government with regard to the restructuring of certain industries and companies. It is therefore at the centre of many industrial developments in the Netherlands. The Government owns about 50% of the shares of the National Investment Bank.

Ireland

There is a long-established venture capital community including five private-sector funds and two semi-State bodies with small business units. Exit routes used are the Dublin Stock Exchange and the London USM, where the shares of some 20 Irish companies are traded. In total, about £30 million of venture capital has been invested in nearly 100 companies since the early 1970s – most of which have grown entirely within the Irish economy.

The five private-sector funds are described below.

Allied Irish Investment Bank

The Allied Irish Investment Bank (AIIB), which is a subsidiary of Allied Irish Banks Limited, one of the major clearers in Ireland, manages three separate venture or development capital funds.

The first, Allied Combined Trust (ACT), was set up in 1973 and is 51% owned by AIIB. The other shareholders are Irish Life Assurance Company, with 20%, New Ireland Assurance Company, with 20%, and Esso Pension Fund with 9%. The initial capital base of the fund was Ir£0.5 million, but this is increased as necessary, as new investment opportunities arise, by the shareholders providing loan stock. On realisation of an investment, the loan stock may be redeemed.

The principal investment focus of ACT is on private companies in Ireland which are making profits of at least Ir£100,000 per annum but need additional capital to take them through the next stage of their growth. Investments are in the Ir£250,000 and upwards range in return for significant minority stakes (at least 20%). ACT seeks to play an active part in the development of portfolio companies and always requires board representation.

Most recently, in response to encouragement from the IDA, which is anxious to promote a more active private-sector capital market in Ireland, AIIB has launched a new fund, the First Venture Fund (FVF). The policy of this fund is to invest mainly in small-to-medium-sized Irish-based enterprises which offer above average growth potential. There was a partial closing of the fund on 30 September 1983, when a total of over Ir£3 million had been raised from outside sources. AIIB will contribute 25% of the total capital, so the final total is in excess of Ir£4 million.

Avenue Investment Company

Avenue Investment Company is a privately owned industrial investment group which has been active in backing new and developing business ventures in Ireland over the past ten years. Its shareholders are principally members of the McGrath, Duggan and Freeman families, descendants of the original investors in the Irish Glass Bottle Co. and Waterford Glass, both of which are now publicly quoted companies.

Established as an investment company in the earlier years of this century, Avenue first started to diversify out of its traditional glass industry base in the early 1970s. It takes signficant minority (or occasionally majority) equity participations in companies that are at an early stage in their development and provides a considerable amount of management support.

The portfolio has now reached a relatively mature state, comprising a total of 10–12 companies, and no new investments were made during 1983 and 1984. Two of the early investments have been realised at a profit to the group, one through a buy-back by the original entrepreneurs and another through a trade sale.

Development Capital Corporation

Development Capital Corporation (DCC) was set up in May 1976. The initial capital raised for the venture capital fund was Ir£1 million, which was subscribed by ten insurance companies and pension funds and the Ulster Bank Group. Four subsequent rights issues increased the total capital raised to just under Ir£8 million and broadened the shareholder base considerably.

There are now approximately 30 institutional shareholders, including most of the major insurance companies and larger privately funded pension schemes in Ireland. The largest individual shareholder is the Bank of Ireland group, with 20% of the equity.

The company has modelled itself very much on a typical US venture capital partnership. DCC seeks to play a significant part in managing the growth of the companies it backs and one of its senior executives is always nominated to the board of investee companies.

In its early years, DCC invested mainly in established companies but then moved more towards start-ups and early-stage financings. Its portfolio now contains a mix of companies, 19 in all, that are at various stages of development. Most of these are in Ireland, but some investments have been made in the United States, including investments in two venture capital funds managed by Hambrecht and Quist.

Industrial Credit Company

The role of the Industrial Credit Company (ICC) has changed a number of times since it was established in 1933, in the light of changes in economic circumstances and in Government support mechanisms for industry.

Since the 1960s, ICC has acted as a national development bank with 99% of its share capital held by the State. Its main activity is the provision of medium- and long-term loans to new and existing enterprises, with particular emphasis on medium- and small-sized firms. While seeking to make a commercial return, it fulfils its Development Bank role by providing appropriate equity/loan and joint-venture packages to assist the growth of viable companies.

While the main emphasis is on loan finance, ICC sometimes seeks an equity involvement. It has taken this position in order to help the companies in which it invests to expand their business faster than they could otherwise do.

With a maximum equity stake of 19.9%, ICC seeks to establish a beneficial working relationship with its portfolio companies rather than an active involvement in day-to-day management. In many cases it appoints a director.

ICC currently has equity investments in about 80 companies, of which over half are private. The total value of this portfolio is Ir£4.2 million. New investments in private companies are being made at the rate of about eight per year, and the average amount invested per company in 1982/83 was Ir£65,000.

The Investment Bank of Ireland

The Investment Bank of Ireland (IBI), which was established as the merchant banking arm of the Bank of Ireland in 1966, was the first organisation to set up a specialist venture capital investment vehicle in Ireland. This was Share and Loan Trust (SALT), which was formed in 1967 with a capital base of Ir£3 million. IBI contributed 77% of the capital and the balance was put up by ten insurance companies, from both Eire and the United Kingdom. There has been no further injection of capital to the fund, which now has a balance sheet value of Ir£6 million.

SALT seeks to back established private companies seeking long-term finance for further development. The maximum equity stake taken is usually 20% and board representation is not required. Investments are in the range Ir£50,000 to Ir£500,000, with two or three new investments being made per year, mostly at the lower end of this size range.

The Irish Government announced in 1985 new initiatives to revive the National Enterprise Agency (the BTG's equivalent in Ireland) and to establish a National Development Corporation. The National Board of Science and Technology is beginning to focus, after six years of operation, on the smaller-business sector. The Innovation Centre in Limerick is a local government initiative to improve the translation of academic ideas into commercial applications.

Belgium

Apart from being the seat of the EVCA, Belgium is also active in venture capital, with its own association of venture capital funds. There are also State-backed venture capital companies in Belgium for each of the two parts of the country – Flanders and Wallonia.

Private-sector activity

In Belgium several companies exist whose object is to contribute risk capital to small businesses – in some cases through venture capital operations, with a real participation in the management of the business and a return based to a large extent on medium-term appreciation, and sometimes by more conventional financing operations. Most of these companies have derived from major national holding companies:

– Investco, a 60.7% subsidiary of Almanij, had funds of its own amounting to 698 million Belgian francs (£10m) at end–1984.
– Prominvest, set up in 1973 and owned by Groupe Bruxelles Lambert and Société Nationale d'Investissement (SNI), had funds amounting to 638 million francs (£9m) at end–1984. During 1984, 24 proposals (out of more than 140 investigated) led to investments amounting to a total of 364 million francs (£5m), with Prominvest participating in the setting up of 11 companies, subscribing six increases in capital and acquiring an interest in seven enterprises by purchasing the shares of existing shareholders.
– Regio is owned by Ibel (50%) and Mosane (50%), two companies of the Copeba Group.
– UFI and VIV are two regional branches of the Société Générale de Belgique, which owns 75.25% and 86.75%, respectively, of their capital.

Advent: In December 1982, two companies were formed simultaneously: Advent Belgium, responsible for obtaining and investing funds, and Advent Management Belgium, whose role is to manage the holdings. Advent Belgium, whose capital rose from 300 million to 500 million francs (£4–7m) during the course of 1983, has a broad institutional body of shareholders, with the majority of shares Belgian-owned. Besides Sofina, which owns 32.8% of the capital (directly and indirectly via Rebelco), there is the Dutch group Oranje-Nassau (25%), Investco (19%), the AG Group, Assubel, Royale Belge and Hennex (4% each), the VIV, and the French insurance group Drouot (together owning 7.2%). The object of Advent Management Belgium is to promote industrial activities in Belgium based on technological innovation. These activities may be carried on by new enterprises or by older companies wishing to launch a new process or product.

Public-sector initiatives

Besides these private companies, public authorities have also been responsible for various initiatives concerning small businesses.

– The SNI has a very broad portfolio of holdings.

– Apart from its role as agent and technical adviser to the Flemish region and its holdings, particularly in the field of high technology, the GIMV (Gewestelijke Investeringsmaatschappij voor Vlaanderen) also puts up risk capital outside its borders. In 1983 it invested half a million dollars in Columbine Venture Fund, a US venture capital fund established in Denver (Colorado).

– The SRIW (Société Régionale d'Investissement de Wallonie) carries on the same type of activity in the southern region of the country. Its portfolio shows a particular interest in new technologies, which occupy first place with 31% of the total, and in the agricultural/food sector, which amounts to 12% of the total. In the area of venture capital, the SRIW acquired in March 1984 a million-dollar holding in Lambda III, a US fund controlled by Drexel Burnham Lambert, a subsidiary of GBL. Just as in the case of the Columbine Venture Fund operation, the main purpose of the investment in Lambda III is to exploit reverse transfer (to Belgium) of US technology.

The two holding agreements with Columbine and Lambda actually provide for the transfer of technical and financial information that the two funds have available, the maintaining of contracts with the enterprise financed by them, as well as free consultations with the fund managers.

– The SRIB/GIMB (Société Régionale d'Investissement de Bruxelles – Gewestelijke Investeringsmaatschappij van Brussel) has not yet made any investments; its services have in fact been operational only since August 1984. Several proposals are currently being studied.

– There are also the 'Invests', types of mixed holdings (SNI and private capital) set up in order to facilitate the conversion of docks affected by the crisis in iron and steel. Currently numbering eight, these 'Invests' can at present finance any kind of industrial or commercial activity; operations similar to venture capital financing are not excluded.

New legislation

Broadly based on the draft bill regarding high-technology companies, introduced in October 1983 by Melchior Wathelet, the economic recovery law, in its section concerning the promotion of innovating capital, contains a series of provisions to encourage innovating companies and to furnish incentives to the shareholders of these companies.

Denmark

The concept of venture financing was virtually unknown to Danish financial circles until recently. Since 1982, however, the subject has come very much to the fore. Thus, the question of supplying the smaller business with risk-bearing capital has been intensely debated by the public. Furthermore, various practical initiatives have been adopted in order to promote the supply of subordinated loan capital to trade and industry. Finally, a number of companies have been established since 1983 with the aim of venture capital financing.

The very limited interest taken in venture capital financing so far is attributable partly to the high level of Danish interest rates, partly to the incidence of taxation and partly to attitudes among the population and politicians which have not exactly encouraged people to make active, risk-bearing investments or to take the step from wage-earner to independent businessman.

In all these areas, changes have apparently occurred or are occurring which have contributed to creating a greater interest in active investments. Since the end of 1982 interest rates have dropped from 22% to 14%, which has considerably reduced the opportunity costs of making risk investments and improved the profitability of new investments. One result of this is that share prices more than doubled during 1983/84, which has had a cumulative effect on the interest taken in risk investments.

The conditions of taxation – i.e. high personal taxes as well as the relatively lower taxes on non-risk investments – have not so far favoured personal capital formation by investment in shares. Furthermore, the tax rules have so far had a restraining effect on the incentive to establish companies with the purpose of making minority investments. The rules are now being eased in these fields.

Similarly, the rules for institutional investors and private individuals' pension savings have been amended, so that a larger part of the portfolios can now be invested actively, in risk investments.

In 1983 and 1984, several companies were established to supply smaller business concerns with venture capital so that the estimated total value of venture capital in Denmark has reached DKr500 million (£40m) to date.

Since its foundation in 1979, Privatbanken's Initiative Fund has been able to offer subordinated loan capital. Only with the launching of development capital in 1983 – Privatbanken's version of venture capital – has it become possible to make active investments on a large scale in the form of share capital and subordinated loan capital. Since it was started the Initiative Fund has invested DKr58 million (£4m) in new subordinated loan capital investments; with the introduction of development capital, an additional amount of DKr50 million venture capital has been made available to the Fund.

The companies of Dan-Venture A/S and RB-Invest A/S were established in 1982 by a number of banks and savings banks with a view to arranging for the savings of pension funds to be invested actively, namely in unlisted shares. The capital of each company amounts to DKr25 million (£2m). The National Trade Unions Centre (LO) took steps in 1983 to establish the company of Dansk Erhvervsinvestering A/S for the same purpose. The capital is DKr240 million (£20m).

The Borsinformation'company has established the company BCF Venture Capital Trust A/S with a capital of DKr40 million (£3m). The company was introduced through public offering. The same is the case with Difko Partner A/S with a capital of DKr40 million (£3m), which was introduced recently. In addition to this, several smaller companies have been founded on a private basis for venture capital financing.

It is still too early to analyse the results of these initiatives, as so far the above companies have made only a small number of investments. However, it may be concluded that there is no shortage of risk-bearing capital in Denmark at present. On the basis of the venture financing offers that have appeared during 1984, it may be estimated that in the short term a further DKr300–400 million (£30m) can be provided in the form of venture capital, from liquidity already raised.

Italy

The venture capital industry here is in its infancy and is difficult to distinguish from the extensive network of State financial incentives for industry – particularly in the southern half of the country.

Greece

There is no real venture capital market yet, as distinguished from substantial government aid to industry.

Sweden

Venture capital is rarely found in the non-EEC countries of Europe; the notable exception is Sweden, where a recent burgeoning in venture capital has taken place. More than ten funds have been launched in the past two years, to join the few in existence for a decade or more. There is now a share market for small firms, launched in 1983.

Future European trends

There are some fundamental obstacles in the way of European venture capital growth.

Limited exit routes

Apart from the United Kingdom, with its full stock market listings, USM, OTCs and an active institutional private placement market, Europe's venture capitalists do not yet have an effective realisation point in their own countries. Since some form of share quotation is a key step in generating liquidity for the industry – as well as enabling comparative fund performance to be measured – the development of effective exit markets will be fundamental to the progress of most countries' venture capital movements. It has been suggested by the writer at various conferences that London, with its highly effective securities trading systems – now comparable to those in the United States – should become Europe's venture capital exit market. Whether this simple solution would overcome the national pride of other Europeans is a matter for conjecture.

Technological diffusion

The US electronics industry, responsible for so many venture capital successes, is concentrated in two main centres – California and Massachusetts. In Europe, there are many centres where governments have seduced young high-technology firms to set up, with grants and special regional schemes.

No single area of Europe remotely resembles the concentration of technological expertise in the US electronics centres or the ability of small high-tech companies to feed off each other's products; facilities and personnel are seriously limited in Europe. Mini-centres in Europe which show some signs of growing into concentrations of technology are Cambridge University Science Park (with 400 high-tech companies in its catchment area), Silicon Corridor (Reading, Newbury, Swindon) and Silicon Glen in Fife – all in the United Kingdom – together possibly with Toulouse in France and Munich in West Germany.

European governments are largely to blame for this unsatisfactory state of affairs since they interfere, through their regional policies, with the market mechanisms – thus preventing the potential magnets of excellence from attracting the right kind of entrepreneurial outfits, and thereby enhancing the businesses already clustered there. Basically, there are too many competing would-be centres of technological excellence in Europe at the present time, and Europe's technology is consequently far too widely diffused to provide the rapid market response mechanism needed to answer the North American and Japanese challenge – and to realise the market potential from the many technological 'firsts' achieved throughout Europe.

Purchasing discrimination

Throughout Europe, it is difficult for small companies to become key component, service or sub-assembly suppliers to large companies and thus benefit from the scale of growth potential available with large companies' sheer size of demand. Small companies' cash flows are specifically discriminated against by large companies' credit control policies. New products or services launched by new or small companies are not perceived to carry the same 'quality assurance' as those provided by the subsidiaries of large companies. The reverse is true in North America.

Public purchasing policies in the United States are also attuned to equal opportunity for the smaller suppliers, and in some cases, positive discrimination is made in favour of small businesses. In Europe, it is difficult for the smaller company to become a significant supplier to the State or to public utilities, competing against the larger, better-established businesses. The small business can usually prosper only by becoming an indirect supplier to the State through the large companies which, as noted, are difficult customers.

Cultural prejudice

As discussed in relation to the United Kingdom (Chapter 12), Europe is still prejudiced against the small business entrepreneur, and experienced managers do not yet have the equity incentives to tempt them away from the safe and prestigious large companies for which they currently work.

The future

Continental European cultures are perhaps even more risk-averse than the British culture. There is a real danger that top-down, State-led venture capital will lead their entrepreneurs away from the single goal of profit maximisation which so clearly separates the US entrepreneur from his transatlantic fellows. That said, the recent strong trend in continental Europe towards a State-independent venture capital community can only be encouraging.

There is much going on in cross-border venture capital matters, as between UK and continental European venture capital funds. as well as signs of a few US funds venturing into 'the wider Europe'. All this can only be to the good of the European entrepreneur.

Annexes Deal structures

Introduction

The annexes which follow cover a range of deal structures in venture capital investments, based on actual cases seen at Equity Capital for Industry (ECI). The emphasis throughout is on the capital structure at the time of the transaction, rather than on the profit/loss or cash flow financing implications. A whole volume would be required to do justice to an examination of the other factors that flow from a particular deal structure – not least, of course, the actual post-investment performance of the business itself. This section is not concerned with valuation of the business (see Chapter 9) and hence the phrase *equity* is used, to include both the nominal share value and any share premium resulting from shares being issued at a higher than nominal value – but the venture capitalist and the founder/entrepreneur must clearly agree on this key matter for any deal to be possible at all.

In the examples of deal structures that follow, it is assumed that any cash injection into the business is consumed for expansion/ development purposes – even though, on day one, the actual cash will of course go directly into the business's bank account and thereby reduce borrowings. The '*after*' structures are representative of the position after the amount raised has been used in the business. A more accurate picture, in accounting terms, is only likely to complicate an appreciation of these basic, and stylised, capital structures.

It is important, in viewing these deal structures, to bear in mind the description of the various financing instruments, summarised at the beginning of Chapter 3.

The author is indebted to Patrick Taylor of Coopers & Lybrand, who has cast a critical accountant's eye over the examples, which are simplified formats of the actual structures in each 'live' case.

Annexe 1 Early-stage financing

1A   Seed capital

The first basic options with a 'seedcorn' or seed capital deal structure are:

(a) to fund the project with a largely debt-based package, preserving the entrepreneur's equity control;

(b) to develop a largely equity package, where the founder's equity position is diluted by outside equity partners, and where the initial borrowings are kept to a minimum.

The advisability, or otherwise, of an early-stage project being largely debt-based is discussed in Chapter 12, but few seed capital projects can afford the financing costs of a debt-based deal structure. Two alternative structures are shown below:

	£000
Capital required:	
preliminary costs	30
licensing/patent fees	15
premises/equipment	30
working capital	70
(incl. salaries, overheads, etc.)	
prototype construction	15
contingencies	25
consultancy fees	25
	210

Debt-based structure		Equity-based structure
£000		£000
50	Founders' ordinary shares	50
–	Investors' ordinary shares*	50
50	Total equity	100
60	Medium-term loan (80% Govt guarantee)	60
100	Bank overdraft	50
160	Borrowings	110
320%	Debt: % Equity	110%

* Investors' shares likely to be preferred ordinary shares with prior income and repayment rights. Also, investors' shares likely to carry first option on follow-up financings.

1B   Start-up

Frequently the founder will have exhausted his own resources in pulling his business through the pre-start-up or seed capital stage without recourse to outside help. The equity base of the business has been eroded through the pre-start-up losses. There is thus a requirement for new investors to enable the business to reach commercialisation and achieve profitability, but the entrepreneur is concerned to minimise his own equity dilution. Assuming an extra £450,000 is needed to bring the business into full-scale operation, and that the founder is not prepared to surrender control (Structure A only), a possible deal structure could be:

Before		After (Structure A)	After (Structure B)
£000		£000	£000
75 (100%)	Founders' ordinary equity	75 (60%)	75 (33%)
(325)	Revenue deficit	(325)	(325)
–	Investors' preferred ordinary shares	50 (40%)	175 (67%)
–	Investors' redeemable preference	300	175
	Shares (participating in profits)		
(250)	Total equity	100	100
250	Bank debt (founders' guarantee)	150	150
	Investors' subordinated loan stock* (no guarantee)	100	100
250	Borrowings	250	250
Negative borrowing base	Debt: % Equity – gross	250%	250%
	– net of investors' debt	150%	150%

* Subordinated debt ranks after all creditors, and ahead of only preference and ordinary capital.

Structure A

The objective of leaving the founder with control has been achieved, and to reward the new investors for taking the major equity risk with £350,000 (compared with the entrepreneur's £75,000) for only a 40% minority equity position, they will have the right to a fixed dividend and to share the profits before any ordinary dividends are paid. Borrowings remain high, but the profits breakthrough is possibly near, from which time second-round equity (and debt funding) should be available. Often the new investors will also be prepared to refinance some of the borrowings through unsecured or subordinated loan stock, as shown in the example above.

Structure B

Here, the new investors are tougher, and require a higher share of the equity to provide them with adequate reward for their risks; they still receive an equity reward on only half their equity injection, and they may also have £100,000 of loan stock at risk.

'Greenfield' structure

A more unusual start-up structure is as shown below for a 'greenfield' operation, where one of the partners has already carried out the seed capital investment and, because of the location, generous grants/loans may be available from the UK Government and the EEC (ECSC or EIB loan).

	£000
Total project cost = £2.5 million	
Investors:	
Founder/investors' 'A' ordinary shares*	50
Industrial partners' 'B' ordinary shares*	500
Venture capitalists' 'C' ordinary shares*	1,050
Total equity	1,600
Department of Industry grants	200
ECSC loan (subsidised interest)**	500
EEC grants	200
	2,500

* The difference between these three classes of shares is that of income rights (if any) to dividends, and priority rights in any liquidation. The 'C' shares will rank ahead of the 'B' shares in these respects, and the 'B' shares ahead of the 'A' shares.
** This loan would be guaranteed by a recognised UK bank.

1C   Second-round

At this stage the business is usually in profit, if only just, and the forward development is held back because the start-up financing has been exhausted – even though there may be no borrowings.

Structure A

Assuming the business is in profit, but that £500,000 is needed for forward development, a possible structure is:

Before £000		After £000
50 (100%)	Founders' ordinary equity	50 (70%)
200	Revenue retentions	200
–	Investors' ordinary shares	100 (30%)
–	Investors' (convertible) preference shares*	150
250	Total equity	500
–	Government Loan Guarantee Scheme**	75
–	Medium-term (5- or 7-year) bank loan (secured)	175
–	Borrowings	250
Nil	Debt: % Equity	50%

* Probably participating in profits and redeemable over, say, ten years and also possibly convertible into ordinary shares.
** Loan Guarantee Scheme rules have tightened and may not allow for lending to a profitable company.

Although the founder has raised twice the net worth of his business, he still retains 70%, with the new equity partner(s) holding 30%. This is possible partly because of the healthy equity base in the business, the seed capital and start-up stages having been overcome successfully, and partly because the new equity partners' injection (at a premium over par value) has doubled this equity base, enabling half the financing to be in debt form without over-gearing the young business.

Structure B

A second-round financing is not always such a straightforward case. Where the business is not yet in profit and the start-up finances are exhausted, even though there may be little borrowing, a structure to raise £470,000 could be:

Before £000		After £000
10 (15%)	Founders' ordinary equity	10 (10%)
300 (85%)	Start-up partners' ordinary shares	300 (45%)
(400)	Revenue deficit	(400)
–	Second-round investors' ordinary shares	300 (45%)
(90)	Total equity	210
30	Bank borrowings (secured)	200
(60)	Negative borrowing base	
	Debt: % Equity	95%

Here, the original managers were active members of a start-up consortium involving sleeping partners who provided most of the start-up finance in return for an 85% shareholding. The start-up proved slower than expected to move into profit, and a further round of finance is required – which the original investors cannot provide. The incoming investors are thus able to invest on the same terms as the original investors, leaving each group with around a 45% shareholding and the management retaining 10%, at a less painful dilution (of a third) than suffered by their sleeping partners (of nearly a half) from 85% down to 45%. The different degree of dilution is achieved by the price paid for the second-round issue of ordinary shares equalling that paid by the sleeping partners at the first round. At the second round, additional founders' shares are then made available to the management, to maintain their motivation at the original level – whatever the composition of that management team, where changes may be required by the incoming second-round investors.

Annexe 2 Later-stage financing

2A Expansion

At the later stages of development, a business can afford to service its new equity from the outset, and thus a multi-layer deal structure is frequently used. Rarely will the entrepreneur have to concede more than a minority equity position to the new investors – apart from major acquisitions, where the business may double or even triple in size. Here are two cases of expansion financing:

Structure A – organic development

The business involved had grown from its start with only borrowed money, and although it had built up substantial retained profits, its bankers were not prepared to fund the next significant step, a £1,000,000 extension of the business into new markets together with the construction of a modern warehouse.

Before £000		After £000
1,000 (100%)	Founders' ordinary equity	1,000 (75%)
1,000	Revenue retentions	1,000
–	New investors' ordinary shares	500 (25%)
–	New investors' preference shares	500
2,000	Total equity	3,000
3,000	Borrowings	3,000
150%	Debt: % Equity	100%

The entrepreneur retains a 75% equity position and the new investor has 25%, but also the right to participate in profits through his preference shares, which may also have conversion rights into ordinary shares.

Structure B – acquistion

Sometimes in venture capital, an existing portfolio company has the opportunity to acquire a business larger than itself, frequently from another (parent) company with which the business being sold no longer fits. The original venture capital fund is rarely able wholly to finance such a deal itself, so new investors are frequently invited in. Assume the net worths of the respective businesses are: Purchaser £1 million; Acquisition £3 million.

Before £000		After £000
300 (100%)	Founders' equity (incl. original venture capitalists)	300 (50%)
700	Revenue retentions	700
–	New investors' preferred shares	1,000 (50%)
–	New investors' preference shares	1,000
1,000	Total equity	3,000
Nil	Borrowings	1,000
	Debt: % Equity	33%

By sufficiently enlarging the equity base to use debt for part of the acquisition financing, the original investors' equity holding is reduced only by half (to 50%), despite the tripling in size of the business. It should be noted that frequently the net worth of the acquired business, its purchase price and the amount raised from investors by the acquiring company are all different amounts. The ensuing structures can take a whole range of alternative shapes. The example here is an actual illustration of one real-life investment. The preferred shares could also have had variable conversion rights into ordinary shares, depending upon the profit performance of the business over, say, a 2–5-year period.

2B   Replacement

A frequent form of later-stage financing in the pre-USM/OTC era (before 1980), this form of investment is much less common today. It is, however, sometimes the case at a pre-quotation stage that an expansion financing is combined with some 'money out' for the founder-entrepreneur. Usually, the ordinary shares being sold by the entrepreneur will be switched into some form of preferred equity. Assuming the realisation of a 10% shareholding for £500,000, plus the raising of a further £2 million of expansion finance, the deal structure could be:

Stage 1 – 10% replacement (money out)

Before £000		After £000
100 (100%)	Founders' equity	90 (90%)
1,000	Revenue retentions	1,000
–	New investors' preferred shares*	10 (10%)
1,100	Total equity	1,100
500	Borrowings	500
45%	Debt: % Equity	45%

* Converted from 'old' founders' ordinary shares into 'new' preferred ordinary shares to give the new investors priority rights to income and to the proceeds of any future liquidation.

The new investors will have paid the founders significantly in excess of nominal value for the 10% shareholding, but this will only be reflected in the founders' own bank accounts. The business itself will derive no benefit until the injection of £2 million expansion finance, which would usually be a simultaneous exercise.

Stage 2 – £2 million expansion financing (money in)

Before £000		After £000
90 (90%)	Founders' equity	90 (60%)
1,000	Revenue retentions	1,000
10 (10%)	New investors' preferred shares	510 (40%)
–	New investors' preference shares	1,500
1,100	Total equity	3,100
500	Borrowings	500
45%	Debt: % Equity	16%

The new investors have achieved a fair deal on the expansion financing element, although they had to accept an equivalent to USM valuation for the 'money out' element in Stage 1. The £1.5 million of preference shares will probably carry participation rights as well as a fixed coupon.

2C   Turnaround

The turnaround is not yet seen as often in the United Kingdom as it is in the United States. In effect, a turnaround deal structure much resembles a start-up or second-round financing, where the business is not yet profitable but over-borrowed. The key difference is that turnarounds are often found in mature businesses with undramatic growth potential once the turnaround is achieved, and whose management will also need some restructuring, whatever the deal structure itself. Although this is not common, the case below had offers both from an institutional consortium of venture capitalists and from BES (Business Expansion Scheme) funds:

Before		After Venture capital	After BES
£000		£000	£000
100 (100%)	Founders' equity	100 (49%)	100 (51%)
200	Revenue retentions	200	200
–	New investors' ord. shares	200 (51%)	700 (49%)
–	New investors' convertible preference shares	100 (15%)	–
300	Total equity	600	1,000
1,000	Bank debt	300	300
–	Investors' subordinated debt	100	–
1,000	Borrowings	400	300
330%	Debt: % equity – gross	67%	30%
	– net	50%	

In the venture capital alternative it can be seen that the new investors have a controlling position – 51% from the outset, plus the probability of an extra 15% arising from conversion of the preference shares. Existing investors in a turnaround normally have to suffer loss of control by virtue of the amount of new equity required. The BES route may not involve so heavy a dilution of the founders' equity position because of the ability of BES funds to use the tax benefit to their investors as the basis for a higher valuation of the business. In both cases, bank debt is reduced by £700,000 (to £300,000), but the venture capitalists are also prepared to offer subordinated debt.

A different structure can be achieved through a more equity-orientated deal than the one above, where the debt is still substantial, although less so under the BES proposal.

Annexe 3 Buy-outs

3A Small-scale corporate sale

When a buy-out is based on the acquisition of a business from its parent company by its own management team, the transaction can take various forms. The share capital (and liabilities) of the business may be purchased, or solely the assets and trading rights. In either case, the structure of the deal will depend, among other issues, on the valuation of the assets being purchased and whether they are all required in the newly independent business. For example, if certain assets can be realised within a relatively short period (say 12 months), then the deal structure can include a higher proportion of debt than where no asset realisation is possible. In the latter case, a debt-orientated deal structure is not ideal for the newly independent business, since its initial gearing may well prevent financing flexibility if the growth of the business requires recourse to conventional sources of borrowing. It may also provide inadequate safety margins for new borrowings in the event that performance falls below the business plan expectations.

Another basic feature of buy-outs is the management's shareholding. In most cases where the purchase consideration exceeds £1 million, the management team is unlikely to be able to negotiate a controlling interest, at least not initially.

The deal structures illustrated below cover debt-financed or asset-leveraged buy-outs and also those where an equity-financed route is preferable. The illustrations do not embrace the complex issues of tax structures and methods of transferring assets from the vendor parent company to the new buy-out company. Many excellent sources of advice on this variable, but important, aspect of buy-outs already exist, particularly in the accounting and legal professions. Each case has its own peculiarities and a separate book could be based solely on this aspect of buy-outs.

Debt-based small-scale buy-out (cost £1 million)

Assuming asset disposals possible:

Before asset disposals £000		After asset disposals £000
50	Management ordinary shares	50
100	Investors' convertible participating preferred ordinary shares (CPPOs)	100
100	Investors' redeemable preference shares	100
250	Total equity	250
500	Investors' loan stock	–
250	Bank debt	250
750	Borrowings	250
300%	Debt: % equity	100%

Here the investors have funded the short-term debt portion of the package in the expectation of their loan stock being repaid on the sale of surplus assets – which may take the form of a sale and leaseback to a savings institution. The management's equity holding will vary depending on its negotiating position and on the venture capitalists' philosophy. It is increasingly common for the management's eventual holding in a buy-out to vary according to its profit performance over a pre-set time period, say 3–5 years. In the example above, with a commitment of £50,000 from a long-term equity requirement of £250,000, i.e. 20% of the total, it is possible that management's initial holding would be a majority stake of, say, 55%, with an incentive to hit its profit targets – based on an increasing conversion rate by the investors' CPPOs, to the extent that management's profit targets are not met, which has the effect of reducing management's stake, probably on a 'ratchet' or 'earn-out' formula, down to 40% minimum.

The ratchet or earn-out means that the CPPO will convert into relatively more ordinary shares, the greater the shortfall of profit achievement over a 2–5-year period – on a negotiated, pre-agreed scale. The ratchet often works in the opposite direction, where to the extent that the initial profit targets are exceeded, the management team can achieve a higher equity stake.

Equity-based small-scale buy-out (cost £1 million)

Assuming no asset disposals possible:

Equity buy-out £000		Debt buy-out £000
50 (40%)	Management ordinary shares	50 (55%)
50 (40%)	Investors' ordinary shares	50 (25%)
200 (20%)	Investors' CPPOs	50 (20%)
200	Investors' red. pref. shares	100
500	Total equity	250
–	Investors' loan stock	250
500	Bank debt	500
500	Borrowings	750
100%	Debt: % equity	300%

Equity buy-out

Here the investors have taken a position equal to management in ordinary shares to keep the equity base relatively unborrowed, to allow for further conventional (overdraft) borrowing as the company grows. It is likely that the investors (a group of more than one – in a syndicate) will have a controlling shareholding, at least initially, by inclusion of their CPPO rights.

Debt buy-out

There are no asset disposal possibilities, but the debt package includes a high gearing at the outset, which clearly has a depressive effect on profits due to the high servicing cost of the debt. The investors' share-holding position, however, is likely to be reduced to a minority participation as the investors have less equity at risk, at least in theory, with £200,000 as opposed to £450,000 in the equity buy-out example. In practice, of course, the investors' loan stock is probably uncovered by disposable assets and thus amounts to an equity exposure – without the equity reward.

Deferred consideration buy-out

Where the vendors can be persuaded to leave in part of their consideration, preferably at nil interest, for several years, the external debt element in the structure can be reduced.

	£000
Management's ordinary shares	60 (60%)
Investors' ordinary shares	40 (40%)
Investors' participating preference shares	100
Investors' redeemable preference shares	100
Total equity	300
Vendors' deferred loan (guaranteed by investors)	300
Bank debt	400
Total borrowings	700
Debt: % equity – gross	233%
– net of deferred loan	133%

3B   Large-scale corporate sale

In many ways similar to a small corporate sale (apart from size), the larger buy-outs are usually syndicated among several investors, whereas the smaller ones are often completed by one, or at most a pair of investors. Most large-scale buy-outs include investors' debt as well as equity, and the syndicate almost always has a controlling position throughout. The management stake can still be subject to a 'ratchet' arrangement, with an eventual equity position dependent upon profit performance.

Large-scale buy-out (cost £5 million)

	£000
Management ordinary shares	200
Investors' preferred ordinary shares	300
Investors' conv. preference shares	500
Investors' redeemable preference shares	1,000
Total equity	2,000
Investors' subordinated loan stock	1,000
Bank loans	2,000
Borrowings	3,000
Debt: % equity	150%

In this case the investors are subscribing £2.8 million compared with the management's £0.2 million, i.e. 56% of the total commitment, compared with the management's 4% and the bank's 40%. It would be usual in such a large deal for the management's shareholding to vary from 25–40%, depending upon profit performance. In a £10 million buy-out, their stake would be correspondingly lower at 10–15% of the eventual equity.

3C   Share repurchase

A less frequent form of buy-out than the more commonly found corporate disposal, share repurchase involves the existing management team – with the help of new external investors – buying out the (usually) controlling holdings of the original founders, who have retired from executive duties or are about to. The operation is usually designed to switch control to the present management team from the original, now 'sleeping', shareholders.

Old company £000		New company £000
70 (70%)	Outgoing ordinary shareholdings	–
30 (30%)	Management ordinary shareholdings	60 (60%)
4,900	Reserves	2,250
–	Investors' ordinary shares	40 (40%)
–	Investors' conv. pref. shares	2,000
–	Investors red. pref. shares	650
5,000	Total equity	5,000
1,000	Borrowings	1,000
20%	Debt: % equity	20%

The outgoing shareholders have received part of the fruits of their early labours through an effective distribution of their retained profits, which have been replaced by an injection of new equity from the incoming investors. Simultaneously, the management team has switched from a 30% minority to a 60% controlling position.

The structure includes convertible preference shares for the investors, to avoid immediate change of control from the outgoing shareholdings to the incoming investors – which would leave management without its desired initial controlling position. There would usually be a 'ratchet' or 'earn-out' mechanism to adjust these initial shareholdings by enhanced conversion rights for the incoming investors, in the event that the management falls short of its own profits projection.

3D   Receivership

A receivership buy-out is more akin in structure to a start-up than to the corporate sale or share repurchase types of buy-out. In essence, a new company is formed to take on the assets and trading names of the group (or part of the group) in receivership. The capitalisation of the new company depends partly on the valuation of assets being acquired. For example, if stocks or properties can be purchased from the receiver at a discount on their realisable value, a higher level of debt can be built in than if a full value is being paid for the assets.

Stage 1 – Receivership buy-out (cost £2 million)

£3m assets purchased for £2m £000	New company	£3m assets purchased for £3m £000
100	Management equity	100
400	Investors' equity	400
500	Total equity	500
1,000	Investors' debt	1,000
500	Bank debt	1,500
1,500	Borrowings	2,500
300%	Debt: % Equity	500%

Stage 2 – After asset realisation

500	Borrowings	500
–	Investors' debt	1,000
500	Bank debt	1,500
500	Borrowings	2,500
100%	Debt: % Equity	500%

Appendices

Appendix A
Major sources of venture capital in the United Kingdom

Members of the British Venture Capital Association are denoted by an asterisk(*).

Aberdeen Fund Managers,
9 Queen's Terrace,
Aberdeen AB1 1XL
Tel. Aberdeen (0224) 631999

Abingworth PLC,*
26 St James's Street,
London SW1A 2HA
Tel. 01-839 6745

Advent Limited,*
25 Buckingham Gate,
London SW1E 6LD
Tel. 01-828 4792

Alan Patricof Associates Ltd,*
24 Upper Brook Street,
London W1Y 1PD
Tel. 01-493 3633

Allied Irish Investment Co. Ltd,*
c/o Pinners Hall,
8–9 Austin Friars,
London EC2N 2AE
Tel. 01-920 9155

Alta-Berkeley Associates,*
25 Berkeley Square,
London W1X 5HB
Tel. 01-629 1550

Bankers Trust,
Dashwood House,
69 Old Broad Street,
London EC2P 2EE
Tel. 01-726 4141

Barclays Development Capital,
Chatsworth House,
66–70 St Mary Axe,
London EC3A 8BD
Tel. 01-623 4321

Baring Brothers Hambrecht and
    Quist,*
8 Bishopsgate,
London EC2N 4AE
Tel. 01-626 5133

Baronsmead Associates Ltd,*
59 London Wall,
London EC2M 5TP
Tel. 01-638 6826

Biotechnology Investments Ltd,*
PO Box 58, St Julian's Court,
St Peter Port,
Guernsey, Channel Islands
Tel. Guernsey (0481) 26741

Birmingham Technology
    Limited,*
Love Lane,
Birmingham B7 4BJ
Tel. 021-359 0981

Britannia Development Capital,
Salisbury House,
Finsbury Circus,
London EC2
Tel. 01-588 2777

British Linen Bank,*
PO Box 49,
4 Melville Street,
Edinburgh EH3 7N2
Tel. 031-226 4071

British Railways Pension Fund,*
50 Liverpool Street,
London EC2P 2BQ
Tel. 01-247 7600

British Technology Group,*
Incorporating National
    Enterprise Board (NEB) and
    National Research
    Development Corporation
    (NRDC),

101 Newington Causeway,
London SE1 6BU
Tel. 01-403 6666

Brown Goldie,
16 St Helen's Place,
London EC3A 6BY
Tel. 01-638 2575

Brown Shipley Development,
Founders Court,
Lothbury,
London EC2R 7HE
Tel. 01-606 9833

Buckmaster & Moore/
    The Second Buckmaster
    Development Fund,*
The Stock Exchange,
London EC2P 2JT
Tel. 01-558 2868

Candover Investments Ltd,*
4–7 Red Lion Court,
London EC4A 3EB
Tel. 01-583 5090

Capital for Companies,
Coverdale House,
14 East Parade,
Leeds LS1 2BH
Tel. Leeds (0532) 438043

Capital Partners International
    Ltd,*
Kingsmead House,
250 Kings Road,
London SW3 5UE
Tel. 01-351 4899/5511

Capital Ventures Ltd,*
Triventure Ltd,
37 London Road,
Cheltenham,
Glos. GL52 6HA
Tel. Cheltenham (0242) 584380

Castle Finance Ltd,
PO Box 53,
Surrey Street,
Norwich NR1 3TE
Tel. Norwich (0603) 22200

Castleforth Fund Managers,
26 St Andrew Square,
Edinburgh EH2 1AF
Tel. 031-556 2555

Causeway Capital,
21 Cavendish Place,
London W1M 9DL
Tel. 01-631 3073

Centaur Communications,
First Floor,
60 Kingly St,
London W1
Tel. 01-439 1305

Centreway Business Expansion
    Scheme,* sponsored by
    Centreway Trust PLC,
1 Waterloo Street,
Birmingham B2 5PG
Tel. 021-643 3941

Charterhouse Japhet Venture
    Fund,*
10 Hertford Street,
London W1Y 7DX
Tel. 01-409 3232

CIN Industrial Investments,*
33 Cavendish Square,
London W1M 0AL
Tel. 01-629 6000

Citicorp Venture Capital Ltd,*
Melbourne House,
33 Melbourne Place,
Aldwych,
London WC2B 4ND
Tel. 01-438 1271/1280

Clydesdale Bank Equity,
30 St Vincent Place,
Glasgow G1 2HL
Tel. 041-248 7070

Colegrave Group,
84 Baker Street,
London W1
Tel. 01-486 4422

Commercial Bank of the Near
    East PLC,
Bank Side House,
107–112 Leadenhall Street,
London EC3A 4AE
Tel. 01-283 4041

Commonwealth Development
    Finance Co.,
Colechurch House,
1 London Bridge Walk,
London SE1 2SS
Tel. 01-407 9711

COSIRA,
141 Castle Street,
Salisbury,
Wilts. SP1 3TP
Tel. Salisbury (0727) 336255

County Bank Development
   Capital,*
11 Old Broad Street,
EC2N 1BB
Tel. 01-638 6000

Dartington & Co.,
Darting Central Offices,
Shinners Bridge,
Dartington,
Totnes, South Devon
Tel. Totnes (0803) 862271

Dawnay Day & Co.,
Friars House,
39–41 New Broad Street,
London EC2 1NM
Tel. 01-588 9191

Development Capital Group,*
88 Baker Street,
London W1M 1PL
Tel. 01-486 5021

East Anglian Securities Trust
   Ltd,*
3 Colegate,
Norwich, Norfolk NR3 1BN
Tel. Norwich (0603) 660931
23 Lower Brook Street,
Ipswich,
Suffolk IP4 1QA
Tel. Ipswich (0473) 213237

Electra Investments Trust PLC,*
Electra House,
Temple Place,
Victoria Embankment,
WC2R 3HP
Tel. 01-836 7766

English & Caledonian
   Investment PLC,*
Cayzer House,
2–4 St Mary Axe,
London EC3A 8BP
Tel. 01-623 1212

Equity Capital for Industry Ltd,*
Leith House,
47–57 Gresham Street,
London EC2V 7EH
Tel. 01-606 1000

ET Trust,
Bank House,
The Paddock,
Handforth,
Wilmslow,
Cheshire SK9 3HQ
Tel. Wilmslow (0625) 532535

European Investments Bank,
69 Pall Mall,
London SW1Y 5ES
Tel. 01-839 3351

First Welsh General Investments
   Trust,
114–116 St Mary Street,
Cardiff CF1 1XJ
Tel. Cardiff (0222) 396131

Foreign & Colonial Management
   Limited,*
1 Laurence Pountney Hill,
London EC4R 0BR
Tel. 01-623 4680

Fountain Development Fund,*
100 Wood Street,
London EC2P 2AJ
Tel. 01-628 8011

Gartmore Investments
    Management,
2 St Mary Axe,
London EC3A 8BP
Tel. 01-623 1212

Granville & Co.,*
27–28 Lovat Lane,
London EC3R 8EB
Tel. 01-621 1212

Gresham Trust,*
Barrington House,
Gresham Street,
London EC2V 7HE
Tel. 01-606 6474

Grosvenor Development Capital
    Ltd,*
Commerce House,
2–6 Bath Road,
Slough,
Berks. SL1 3RZ
Tel. Slough (0753) 32623

Guidehouse,
Vestry House,
Greyfriars Passage,
Newgate Street,
London EC1A 7BA
Tel. 01-606 6321

Guinness Mahon Venture Capital
    Unit,*
32 St Mary Axe Hill,
London EC3P 3AJ
Tel. 01-623 9333

Hafren Investment Finance Ltd,*
Pearl House,
Greyfriars Road,
Cardiff CF1 3XX
Tel. Cardiff (0222) 32955

Hambros Advanced Technology
    Trust Ltd,*
51 Bishopsgate,
London EC2P 2AA
Tel. 01-588 2851

Hill Samuel & Co.,
100 Wood Street,
London EC2
Tel. 01-628 8011

Hoare Candover,
59 St James's Street,
London SW1
Tel. 01-404 0344

Hoare Govett Ltd,
Heron House,
319–325 High Holborn,
London WC1
Tel. 01-404 0344

Hoare Octagon Ltd,
59 St James's Street,
London SW1A 1LB
Tel. 01-408 0828

Hodgson Martin Ventures,
4A St Andrews Square,
Edinburgh EH2 2BD
Tel. 031-557 3560

Innotech,*
28 Buckingham Gate,
London SW1E 6LD
Tel. 01-834 2492

Innvotec,
Agriculture House,
Knightsbridge,
London SW1X 7NJ
Tel. 01-245 1977

Intex Executive (UK),
Chancery House,
53–64 Chancery Lane,
London WC2A 1QU
Tel. 01-831 6925

Investors in Industry,*
91 Waterloo Road,
London SE1 8XP
Tel. 01-928 7822

James Finlay Corporation,
Finlay House,
10–14 West Nile Street,
Glasgow G1 2PP
Tel. 041-204 1321

Kleinwort Benson Development
   Capital Ltd,*
20 Fenchurch Street,
London EC3P 3DB
Tel. 01-623 8000

Larpent Newton & Co. Ltd.*
7th Floor,
18 Breams Buildings,
London EC4A 1HN
Tel. 01-831 9991

Lazard Brothers & Co. Ltd/
Development Capital Group
   Ltd,*
21 Moorfields,
London EC2P 2HT
Tel. 01-588 2721

Leisure Development,
13 Park Street,
Windsor,
Bucks. SL4 1LU
Tel. Windsor (0753) 840181

Leopold Joseph & Son Ltd,
31–45 Gresham Street,
London EC2V 7EA
Tel. 01-588 2323

Manufactures Hanover,
7 Princes Street,
London EC2P 2EN
Tel. 01-600 4585

Mathercourt Securities,
1 Lincoln's Inn Field,
London WC2A 3AA
Tel. 01-831 9001

Mercia Venture Capital Ltd,
126 Colmore Row,
Birmingham B3 3AP
Tel. 021-233 3404

Merseyside Enterprise Board,
3rd Floor,
Royal Liver Buildings,
Liverpool L3 1HT
Tel. 051-236 0221

Midland Bank Equity Group,
47–53 Cannon Street,
London EC4M 5SQ
Tel. 01-638 8861

Midland & Northern,
1 Waterloo Street,
Birmingham B2 5PG
Tel. 021-643 3941

Minster Trust,
Minster House,
Arthur Street,
London EC4R 9BH
Tel. 01-623 1050

Montagu Investment
   Managements,
11 Devonshire Square,
London EC2M 4YR
Tel. 01-626 3434

Morris Stewart-Brown & Co.,
8–9 Giltspur Street,
London EC1A 9DE
Tel. 01-248 2894

MTI Managers Ltd,*
70 St Albans Road,
Watford,
Herts. WD1 1RP
Tel. Watford (0923) 50244

Murray Johnstone Ltd,*
163 Hope Street,
Glasgow G2 2UH
Tel. 041-221 5521

National and Commercial
   Glynns,
26 St Andrews Square,
Edinburgh EH2 1AF
Tel. 031-5562 555

Newmarket Venture Capital,*
57 London Wall,
London EC2M 5TP
Tel. 01-638 4551

Noble Grossart Investment,
48 Queen Street,
Edinburgh, EH2 3NR
Tel. 031-226 7011

Northern Ireland Venture
   Capital,
The Midland Buildings,
Whitlar Street,
Belfast BT15 1JP
Tel. Belfast (0232) 755777

Oakland Management Holding
   Ltd,
Ramsbury House,
High Street,
Hungerford,
Bucks. G17 0LY
Tel. Hungerford (0488) 83555

PA Developments,*
Hyde Park House,
60A Knightsbridge,
London SW1X 7LE
Tel. 01-584 2863/235 6060

Parsons Venture Capital Fund,
100 West Nile Street,
Glasgow G1L 2QU
Tel. 041-332 8791

Pegasus Holdings,
11–15 Monument Street,
London EC3R 8JU
Tel. 01-623 4275

Plant Resources,
35 Hill Road,
Cambridge CB2 1NT
Tel. Cambridge (0223) 322114

Prutec Ltd,
17 Buckingham Gate,
London SW1E 6RN
Tel. 01-828 2082

Pruventure,
142 Holborn Bars,
London EC1N 2NH
Tel. 01-404 5611

Quayle Munro,*
42 Charlotte Square,
Edinburgh EH2 4HQ
Tel. 031-226 4421

Quester Capital Management,
2 Queen Anne's Gate Building,
Dartmoth Street,
London SW1H 9BP
Tel. 01-600 4177

Rainford Venture Capital,
Rainford Hall,
Crank Road,
St Helens,
Merseyside WA11 7RP
Tel. St Helens (0744) 37227

Ravendale Group,
21 Upper Brook Street,
London W1Y 1PD
Tel. 01-629 5983

Rothschild Ventures,
PO Box 185,
New Court,
St Swithins Lane,
London EC4P 4DU
Tel. 01-280 5000

Sabrelance Ltd,
25 Bedford Row,
Holborn,
London WC1R 4HE
Tel. 01-493 3599

The St Helens BES Syndicate,
PO Box 36,
St Helens,
Merseyside
Tel. St Helens (0744) 692578

Sapling North West Ltd,
Suite 103–106,
East Cliff County Office,
East Cliff,
Preston,
Lancs. PR1 3JQ
Tel. Preston (0772) 264382

Schroder (J. Henry) Wagg &
    Co.,*
120 Cheapside,
London EC2V 6DS
Tel. 01-382 6000

Scottish Development Agency,*
120 Bothwell Street,
Glasgow G2 7JP
Tel. 041-248 2700

Seedcorn Capital Ltd,*
The Refuge Building,
20 Baldwin Street,
Bristol BS1 1SE
Tel. Bristol (0272) 272250

Singer & Friedlander,
National Westminster House,
8 Park Row,
Leeds LS1 5BQ
Tel. Leeds (0532) 438073

Smithdown Investments,
15 South Molton Street,
London W1Y 1DE
Tel. 01-408 1502

South Glamorgan Investments,
The Commercial Bank of Wales
    PLC,
114–116 St Mary Street,
Cardiff CF1 1XJ
Tel. Cardiff (0222) 396131

Statham Duff Stoop,
Capital House,
22 City Road,
London EC1
Tel. 01-628 5070

Sumit (Sharp Unquoted Midland
    Investment Trust Ltd),*
Edmund House,
12 Newhall Street,
Birmingham B3 3ER
Tel. 021-236 5801

Thamesdale Investment &
    Finance Co.,
206–210 Bishopsgate,
London EC2
Tel. 01-491 4809

The St James's Venture Capital
    Fund Ltd,*
66 St James's Street
London SW1A 1NE
Tel. 01-493 8111

Thompson Clive & Partners
    Ltd,*
24 Old Bond Street,
London W1X 3DA
Tel. 01-491 4809

Trust of Property Shares PLC,
6 Welbeck Street,
London W1
Tel. 01-486 4684

Ulster Venture Capital,
93 University Street
Belfast BE7 1HP
Tel. Belfast (0232) 228490

Venture Founders Ltd,*
39 The Green,
South Bar Street,
Banbury,
Oxon OX16 9AE
Tel. Banbury (0295) 65881

Venture Link Portfolio
    Management Ltd,*
(part of the Venture Link Group)
6–7 Queen Street,
London EC4N 1SP
Tel. 01-236 6891

S. G. Warburg & Co. Ltd,*
33 King William Street,
London EC4R 9AS
Tel. 01-280 2800

Water Authority Super
    Annuation Fund,*
1 Queen Anne's Gate,
London SW1H 9BT
Tel. 01-222 8111

West Midlands Enterprise Board
    Ltd,
Lloyds Bank Chambers,
75 Edmund Street,
Birmingham B3 3HD
Tel. 021-236 8855

West Yorkshire Enterprise Board
    Ltd,
Purlin House,
Queens Street,
Wakefield,
West Yorkshire WF1 1LE
Tel. Wakefield (0924) 371205

Appendix B
Members of the European Venture Capital Association

* Full Member; ** Associate Member.

Belgium
Advent Management NV,*
Industriepark Keiberg,
Excelsiorlaan 7, bus 4,
1930 Zaventem

Arthur Andersen & Co.,**
Kunstlaan 56,
1040 Brussel

Deloitte, Haskins & Sells,
    European Communities
    Office,**
Avenue Louise 287, bte 7,
1050 Bruxelles

Gewestelijke Investerings-
    maatschappij voor
    Vlaanderen,*
Anneessensstraat 1–3,
2000 Antwerpen

Investco NV,*
Regentlaan 54, bus 2,
1000 Brussel

MSL,**
Avenue Louise 306–310, bte 13,
1050 Bruxelles

Monsanto Europe SA,**
Avenue de Tervuren, 270–272,
1150 Bruxelles

Peat, Marwick, Mitchell & Co.,**
EEC Centre,
Kunstlaan 19 H, bus 1,
1040 Brussel

Prominvest NV,*
Marnixlaan 24,
1050 Brussel

Vlaamse Investerings-
    vennootschap NV,*
Kouter 8,
9000 Gent

Denmark
Privatbankens Initiativfond,*
Torvegade 2,
1400 København K

Eire
Allied Irish Investment Bank
    Ltd,*
Bankcentre PO Box 1128,
Ballsbridge,
Dublin 4

Development Capital
    Corporation Ltd,*
Stillorgan,
Blackrock,
Co. Dublin

ICC Corporate Finance Ltd,*
31–34 Harcourt Street,
Dublin 2

Industrial Development
    Authority Ireland,**
43–47 Lower Mount Street,
Dublin 2

France
Afinnovac,**
148 Boulevard Malesherbes,
75017 Paris

Agrinova,*
128–130 Boulevard Raspail,
75006 Paris

Alan Patricof Associés MMG
    SA,*
67 Rue de Monceau,
75008 Paris

Aprodi,**
89 Avenue Kléber,
75784 Paris

Finovelec SA,*
6 Rue Ancelle,
92200 Neuilly

Idianova SA,*
35 Avenue Franklin Roosevelt,
75008 Paris

Innovest SA,*
Le Sébastopol,
3 Quai Kléber,
67055 Strasbourg

IRDI de Midi-Pyrénées SA,*
64 Rue Raymond IV,
31000 Toulouse

Rhône-Poulenc SA,**
25 Quai Paul-Doumer,
92408 Courbevoie Cedex

Siparex SA,*
122 Rue de Créqui,
69006 Lyon

Sofineti,*
12 Avenue George-V,
75008 Paris

Sofinindex SA,*
51 Rue Saint Georges,
75009 Paris

Sofinnova SA,*
51 Rue Saint Georges,
75009 Paris

Soginnove SA,*
5 Rue Boudreau,
75009 Paris

Sudinova,*
20 Rue de la Bourse,
69002 Lyon

Federal Republic of Germany
Deutsche Wagnisfinanzierungs-
    gesellschaft mbH,*
Ulmenstrasse 37–39,
6000 Frankfurt-am-Main

Industriekreditbank AG/
    Deutsche Industriebank,**
Karl-Theodor-Strasse 6,
Postfach 11 18,
4000 Düsseldorf 1

TVM Techno Venture
    Management GmbH und Co.
    KG,*
Ismaniger Strasse 51,
8000 München 80

Greece
Lybian Greek Investment Co.
    SA,**
2–4 Sina Street,
Athens 135

Italy
Italfinanziaria Internazionale
    SpA,*
Piazza Venezia 5,
00187 Roma

Società Finanziaria di
    Partecipazione SpA,*
Via Saverio Mercadente 9,
00198 Roma

The Netherlands
Bank Itec NV,**
Nassauplein 27,
2585 EC's-Gravenhage

Gilde Venture Fund BV,*
Herculesplein 261A,
3584 AA Utrecht

Holland Venture
    Beheermaatschappij BV,*
Rokin 17,
1012 KK Amsterdam

NMB Venture Partners BV,*
Eekholt 26,
Diemen-Zuid,
Postbus 1800,
1000 BV Amsterdam

Nationale Investeringsbank
    NV,**
Carnegieplein 4,
Postbus 380,
2501 BH's-Gravenhage

Nesbic BV,*
Plantage Middenlaan 62,
1018 DH Amsterdam

Ondernemend Vermogen
    Nederland CV,*
Van Houten Industrieel Park 11,
1381 MZ Weesp

Parcom Beheer BV,*
Carnegieplein 5,
2517 KJ's Gravenhage

United Kingdom
Advent Limited*
Egginton House,
25 Buckingham Gate,
London SW1

Alan Patricof Associates Ltd,*
24 Upper Brook Street,
London W1Y 1PD

Alta Berkeley Associates Ltd,*
25 Berkeley Square,
London W1X 5HB

Barclays Development Capital
  Ltd,*
Chatsworth House,
66–70 St Mary Axe,
London EC3A 8BD

CIN Industrial Investments
  Ltd,*
33 Cavendish Square,
London W1M 0AL

Charterhouse Development Ltd,*
65 Holborn Viaduct,
London EC1A 2DR

Citicorp Development Capital
  Ltd,*
335 Strand,
London WC2R 1LS

County Bank Ltd,*
11 Old Broad Street,
London EC2N 1BB

Equity Capital for Industry Ltd,*
Leith House,
47–57 Gresham Street,
London EC2V 7EH

Granville & Co. Ltd,*
27–28 Lovat Lane,
London EC3R 8EB

Investors in Industry PLC,*
91 Waterloo Road,
London SE1 8XP

Johnson & Johnson Development
  Corporation,**
Runnymede Malthouse,
Runnymede Road,
Egham TW20 9BO

Midland Bank Industrial Finance
  Ltd,*
22 Watling Street,
London EC4M 9BR

Pruventure,*
142 Holborn Bars,
London EC1N 2NH

Scottish Development Finance
  Ltd,*
120 Bothwell Street,
Glasgow G2 7JP

Associate Members from
non-EEC countries

Canada
Idea Corporation,**
Suite 800,
33 Yonge Street,
Toronto,
Ontario M5E 1V3

Spain
Empresa Nacioinal de Innovacion
    SA,**
Pza. Marques de Salamanca 8–2,
Madrid-6

Sociedad Bancaya de Promocion
    Empressarial,**
P. de la Castellana 110,
Madrid-6

Index